A TRADITIONALIST CONFRONTS FASCISM

JULIUS EVOLA

A TRADITIONALIST CONFRONTS FASCISM

SELECTED ESSAYS

TRANSLATED BY E CHRISTIAN KOPFF

LONDON
ARKTOS
2015

Printed in the United Kingdom.

ISBN 978-1-910524-02-2

BIC-CLASSIFICATION
Social & political philosophy (HPS)
Fascism & Nazism (JPFQ)
Nationalism (JPFN)

TRANSLATOR
E Christian Kopff

EDITOR
John B Morgan

COVER DESIGN
Andreas Nilsson

LAYOUT
Tor Westman

ARKTOS MEDIA LTD.
www.arktos.com

CONTENTS

A NOTE FROM THE EDITOR

This volume consists of various essays on the subject of the fascist phenomenon that Evola wrote both before and after 1945. It could be considered as a supplement to Arktos' editions of Evola's primary works on the subject of Italian Fascism and National Socialism, *Fascism Viewed from the Right* and *Notes on the Third Reich*. In 2001, Edizioni Mediterranee of Rome published a volume entitled *Fascismo e Terzo Reich*, which collected these two volumes of Evola's along with a number of other essays by him on various aspects of fascism. *A Traditionalist Confronts Fascism* contains all of these essays, apart from the text of the *Autodifesa* from Evola's trial for subversion in 1951, which is already available in English in the Inner Traditions edition of *Men Among the Ruins*. We have also added two additional essays: 'Scientific Racism's Mistake', which we believe will help to illuminate Evola's oft-misunderstood attitude towards race; and 'Orientations', which is the most concise overview of Evola's conception of a correct traditionalist attitude toward politics.

The original places of publication for the contents of this volume are as follows:

- Orientations: *Orientamenti*, originally published as a pamphlet by Imperium in 1950

- Identity Card: 'Carta d'identità', in *La Torre* 1, 1 February 1930
- Two Faces of Nationalism: 'Due facce del nazionalismo', in *La Vita Italiana*, March 1931
- Paneuropa and Fascism: 'Paneuropa e Fascismo', in *Regime Fascista*, 14 May 1933
- Race and Culture: 'Razza e cultura', in *Rassegna Italiana*, January 1934
- What does the Spanish Falange Want?: 'Che cosa vuole il Falangismo spagnolo', in *Lo Stato*, January 1937
- The Spiritual Meaning of Autarchy: 'Significato spirituale dell'autarchia', in *Corriere Paduano*, 1 March 1938
- Legionary Asceticism: 'Legionarismo ascetico', in *Il Regime Fascista*, 22 March 1938
- Corporation and Roman Fidelity: 'Corporazione e romana fedeltà', in *La Nobilta della Stirpe*, April–May 1938
- Party or Order?: 'Partito od Ordine?', in *Corriere padano*, 2 January 1940
- The Spiritual Bases of the Japanese Imperial Idea: 'Basi spirituali dell'idea imperiale nipponica', in *Asiatica* 6, November-December 1940
- Scientific Racism's Mistake: 'L'equivoco del razzismo scientifico', in *La Vita Italiana*, September 1942
- Critical Observations on National Socialist 'Racism': 'Osservazioni critiche sul «razzismo» Nazionalsocialista', in *La Vita Italiana*, November 1933
- Is Nazism on the Way to Moscow?: 'Il nazismo sulla via di Mosca?', in *Lo Stato*, March 1935
- On the Differences between the Fascist and Nazi Conception of the State: 'Sulla differenze fra la concezione fascista e nazista dello Stato', in *Lo Stato*, April 1941

- Hitler's Table Talks: 'Conversazioni di Hitler a tavola', in *Roma*, 19 March 1953
- A History of the Third Reich: 'Una storia del Terzo Reich', in *Il Nazionale*, 1962
- Hitler and the Secret Societies: 'Hitler e le società segrete', in *Il Conciliatore*, October 1971

The footnotes to the Introduction were added by F. Christian Kopff. The footnotes to the text itself were part of the original texts, if they are unmarked, and those footnotes that were added by me are denoted with an '—Ed.'. Where sources in other languages have been cited, I have attempted to replace them with existing English-language editions. Citations to works for which I could locate no translation are retained in their original language, and a translation of the title is offered in the footnotes. Website addresses for on-line sources were verified as accurate and available during June 2015.

Yet again, I would like to thank Professor Kopff for his outstanding and generous work on this volume, as with its companion volumes.

JOHN B. MORGAN
Budapest, Hungary
August 2015

FOREWORD

BY E CHRISTIAN KOPFF

The 1920s were a fast-changing and productive decade for young Julius Evola (1898–1974). He entered it as Italy's most brilliant member of the Dadaist movement in art and poetry. He then turned to developing a philosophy based on the idea of the Absolute Individual, a being whose freedom was so absolute that he could choose both horns of a logical or moral dilemma. Evola did not, however, become a modern, liberal 'individualist'. On the contrary, having faced the abyss into which modern art and modern life were heading, he became an exponent of the Integral Traditionalism of René Guénon (1886–1951). Liberal individualism often rejects tradition and the transcendent. Guénon argued that transcendence and the one Tradition that stands behind and above the many religious and historical traditions are fundamental for making sense of the world, by revealing the metaphysical source that lies behind material reality. Although Guénon emphasised the spiritual and religious sides of traditionalism, his views had political implications. The modern age seemed to him to exemplify the *kali-yuga*, the Dark Age of Hindu scripture, when the material and sensual overwhelm the spiritual and ascetic, eventually bringing about a universal collapse that gives rise to a new Golden Age. As in every Golden Age, society will be reordered according to the traditional hierarchy and its leaders will combine the traits of both priest and

warrior. The Golden Age begins to degenerate when priests and warriors separate into two classes, as in, for instance, the Hindu *brahmin*
(priest) and *kshatriya* (warrior). Leaders in the later stages belong to
one class or the other. Evola, in his idea of the Absolute Individual,
refused to choose between *brahmin* and *kshatriya*, or to acknowledge
that the *brahmin* was superior to the *kshatriya*, as is taught in modern
Hindu theology. He chose to be both guru and warrior, an ascetic who
was also actively engaged with the modern world.

His first opportunity for engagement came from his friendship with Arturo Reghini (1878–1946). Reghini introduced Evola to
Guénon's insights into the religious traditions of the East, but he was
also intrigued with ancient Rome and its contrast with the modern
world's democratic ideals and plutocratic nature. Given that Benito
Mussolini's Fascist Party had recently come to power, Evola used his
friendship with the Fascist ideologue, Giuseppe Bottai (1895–1959),
with whom he had served in the World War, to publish a series of articles in Bottai's magazine, *Critica Fascista*, in 1926 and 1927 on the idea
of 'pagan imperialism' as a model for the new regime, which had taken
the Roman fasces as its symbol. Evola praised the Roman Empire as
a synthesis of the sacred and the regal, an aristocratic and hierarchical system under a true leader. He rejected the Catholic Church as a
source of religion and morality independent of the state, despite its
antiquity and long tradition, because he saw its universalistic claims
as compatible with and tending toward liberal egalitarianism and humanitarianism, despite its anti-Communist rhetoric.

Evola's articles enjoyed a national *succès de scandale* and he
expanded them into a book, *Imperialismo Pagano* (1928),[1] which provoked a heated debate involving many Fascist and Catholic intellectuals, including, significantly, Giovanni Battista Montini (1897–1978),

---

1   *Imperialismo Pagano* (Rome: Atanór, 1928); English translation: *Heathen Imperialism* (Kemper, France: Thompkins & Cariou, 2007).

who was to become the liberal Pope Paul VI. Meanwhile, Mussolini was negotiating with Pope Pius XI (1857–1939) for a reconciliation in which the Church would give its blessings to his regime in return for the protection of its property and official recognition as the religion of Italy. Italy had been united by the Piedmontese conquest of Papal Rome in 1870 and the Popes had never recognized the new government. So Evola could write in 1928, 'Every Italian and every Fascist should remember that the King of Italy is still considered a usurper by the Vatican.'[2] The signing of the Vatican Accords on 11 February 1929 ended that state of affairs as well as the debate. Both Reghini and Bottai turned against Evola.[3]

Evola's alienation from official Fascism continued until the fall of the regime, but it was not as complete as sometimes asserted. Evola certainly insisted on his intellectual and spiritual independence, but he was also on the lookout for connections with Fascism and other movements that were opposed to what he saw as the forces of modern degeneracy. He expressed his vision in the introduction to a short-lived magazine he published for a few months in 1930 (translated in this volume): 'Our journal, *La Torre* [The Tower], was not founded to produce articles in praise of Fascism and the honourable Mussolini. Neither Fascism nor the honourable Mussolini would know what to do with such praise. This journal was founded to defend *principles* that for us would remain absolutely the same whether we found ourselves in a Fascist regime or a Communist, anarchist, or republican one… *To the extent that Fascism follows and defends these principles, so far we can consider ourselves Fascists. So far and no further.*'

---

2   *Imperialismo Pagano*, p. 40.

3   Richard Drake, 'Julius Evola, Radical Fascism, and the Lateran Accords', *Catholic Historical Review* 74 (1988), pp. 403–319; E Christian Kopff, 'Italian Fascism and the Roman Empire', *Classical Bulletin* 76 (2000), pp. 109–115.

Evola developed close relations with German thinkers and writers who were part of that nation's Conservative Revolution.[4] His travels and talks in Germany, which continued even after the advent of the Third Reich, eventually attracted the attention of the SS, which issued an internal report on Evola. After summarizing three of his lectures, the report concluded, 'The ultimate and secret motivation for Evola's theories and plans must be sought in a revolt of the old aristocracy against today's world, which is totally alienated from the upper class. This confirms the initial German impression: that we are dealing with a "reactionary Roman"... His political plans for a Roman-Germanic Imperium are of a utopian character and moreover very apt to cause ideological confusions. Since Evola is also only tolerated and barely supported by Fascism, it is tactically not necessary to accommodate his tendencies from our side.' In a memo dated 8 August 1938 Himmler himself 'acknowledged the report regarding the lectures of Baron Evola and is in full agreement with the thoughts and recommendations stated in the last paragraph thereof', which recommended ignoring Evola and discouraging his influence in Germany.[5]

In the aftermath of the debate over 'pagan imperialism', Evola decided to go his own way and publish his own magazine to develop and present the principles of a true Right. In fact, ten issues of *La Torre* appeared in the first half of 1930, presenting a principled Integral Traditionalist perspective that was generally consistent with the principles of Fascism, but which also occasionally criticised aspects of the regime, as, for instance, the practice of terrorising political opponents using Fascist toughs banded together as *squadre d'azione* (action squads), popularly known as *gli squadristi* or 'Blackshirts'.

---

4   Armin Mohler, *Die konservative Revolution in Deutschland, 1918–1932* (Stuttgart: Vorwerk, 1950), revised in 1972, 1989, 1994, 1999, 2005; J T Hansen, 'Julius Evola und die deutsche konservative Revolution', *Criticón* 158 (1998), pp. 16–32.

5   H T Hansen, 'Julius Evola's Political Endeavors', in Julius Evola, *Men Among the Ruins* (Rochester VT: Inner Traditions, 2002), pp. 62–63.

Evola also mocked Fascist initiatives such as the 'demographic campaign' to increase Italian births, which he viewed as a classic case of modernity's privileging of quantity over quality. As he noted in his autobiography, *The Path of Cinnabar*,[6] in 1963, Evola began these critiques before developing the sort of political connections that would protect him not so much from polemical debate, which he sought, as from physical violence. Fascist toughs started to harass him and he assembled a bodyguard of like-minded young men to protect him. At the same time he worked to develop positive relationships with a few of the Fascist leaders. As the SS had reported to Heinrich Himmler, Evola was 'only tolerated' by official Fascism and regularly harassed by *gli squadristi*. The working relationships he developed showed his intelligence and daring.

In the early 1930s, when another man might yet have been reeling from the failure of his attempt to prevent the reconciliation of the Catholic Church and the Fascist state, and frightened by attacks by Fascist toughs, Evola found a way to win the support of two important Fascist leaders, Giovanni Preziosi (1881–1945) and Roberto Farinacci (1892–1945). His writings eventually attracted the attention of a third, Benito Mussolini. Both Preziosi and Farinacci followed an independent line and both spent time suffering the Duce's displeasure, but their ideological consistency brought them back into favour over time. Preziosi had served as the editor of a newspaper, *Il Mezzogiorno* [The South], in Naples from 1923 until 1929 before conflicts with Mussolini led to his resignation. For thirty years he edited *Vita Italiana* [Italian Life]. During its first two years, from January 1913 to December 1914, it was called *La Vita Italiana all'estero* [Italian Life Abroad] and was initially aimed at Italian immigrants in the United States. The rise of Italian nationalism during the War changed Preziosi's perspective

---

6   Julius Evola, *The Path of Cinnabar: An Intellectual Autobiography* (London: Arktos, 2010); Italian: *Il Cammino del Cinabro: Nuova edizione* (Rome: Mediterranee, 2014).

and he dropped the reference to 'abroad' in the title. Over time the magazine assumed a certain cultural importance within Italy despite its restricted readership because the Duce allowed Preziosi to express his own views, which represented the position popularly known as 'clerical fascism'. From 1931 to 1943 Preziosi permitted Evola to write freely exploring traditionalist themes as long as he did not explicitly contradict Mussolini, whom Evola often mentions with approval. *Vita Italiana* published one of Evola's most controversial articles, 'Scientific Racism's Mistake' (translated in this volume). With the publication in two volumes of Evola's contributions to *Vita Italiana* we can see just how widespread and serious Evola's reading and outreach were during this period.[7]

Perhaps even more important and politically savvy was Evola's relations with Roberto Farinacci. Farinacci's political base was Cremona, where he was *Ras*, Etruscan for 'leader'. Mussolini's title, *Duce*, came from the Latin *Dux*. Fascist leaders like Farinacci and Italo Balbo wanted a title older than the Roman Empire and even the Roman Republic. Farinacci was identified with the 'action squads' and their favourite prank, forcing castor oil down the throat of anti-fascists. The technique 'taught people a lesson' without killing them, and so set a rather different tone from the other, more murderous totalitarianisms. Eventually they went too far and in 1924, *squadristi* murdered the Socialist representative, Giacomo Matteotti. Farinacci was elected head of the Fascist Party from 1925–1926 and saved the government by cracking down on the squads. (He also defended the murderers in court, where three leading Fascists were convicted but later pardoned by the King.) He returned to Cremona in 1926, but remained active, fighting in the Ethiopian War in 1935, when he again held a seat on the Fascist Grand Council. In 1937 he fought in the Spanish Civil War. He

---

7   Julius Evola, *I testi di La Vita Italiana*, 2 vols. (Padova: Libreria AR, 2006).

was one of the stalwarts who refused to vote against Mussolini during the coup engineered by the King on 25 July 1943.

Farinacci was the right patron at the right time. It was hard to question Evola's fascist *bona fides* once he was allied with Farinacci, so *gli squadristi* left him alone. And Farinacci found the perfect post for Evola: editing the cultural 'op ed' page of Farinacci's newspaper, *Regime Fascista*, in Cremona. The newspaper had a reputation as the cutting edge of Fascist thought and policy, but Evola filled the cultural page with the leading intellectual lights of Integral Traditionalism and the German Conservative Revolution. Guénon published there, at first under a pseudonym, but later under his own name. '*La Torre*, purged of its more inflammatory *ad hominem* polemics, thus found a new, safe embodiment in the pages of one of the bastions of Fascist "orthodoxy".'[8] From 1934 to 1943, Farinacci gave Evola a free hand to make *Regime Fascista*'s cultural page a pan-European site for traditionalist ideas and authors.[9]

Evola's interaction with Mussolini stretched over many years. He led the charge against reconciliation with the Catholic Church, which was Mussolini's major domestic achievement. It permitted the integration of the Church and its institutions, including hospitals and schools, into the life of the Italian nation and laid the basis for the Church's political role after the Second World War through the Christian Democratic Party, which dominated Italian politics until 1994. The success of the reconciliation led most Fascists to avoid Evola and even, in some cases, to attack him, but there is good evidence that Mussolini was not angry at him.

A James Gregor believes that Mussolini was favourably disposed to Evola's provocations. 'In retrospect, it is clear that Mussolini allowed

---

8   *The Path of Cinnabar*, p. 112; *Cammino*, p. 201.

9   *Diorama: Problemi dello spirit nell'etica fascista. Antologia della pagina speciale di 'Regime Fascista' diretta da Julius Evola, 1934–35* (Rome: Europa, 1974).

Evola to continue a diversionary controversy with the Church in order to drive the Papacy into the most accommodating arrangement he could. [...] Faced by the apparent threat of a violent anticlerical "fascist" opposition, the Church concluded its negotiations with Mussolini. [...] In part through this deft manipulation of Evola, Mussolini had won what was perhaps his greatest single political success.'[10]

This cynical view may be right, but in conversations with Yvon de Begnac, Mussolini spoke of Evola with respect.[11] For instance, he remarked about the *Pagan Imperialism* debate: 'Despite what is generally thought, I was not at all irritated by Doctor Julius Evola's pronouncements made a few months before the Conciliation on the modification of relations between the Holy See and Italy. Anyhow, Doctor Evola's attitude did not directly concern relations between Italy and the Holy See, but what seemed to him the long-term irreconcilability of the Roman tradition and the Catholic tradition. Since he identified Fascism with the Roman tradition, he had no choice but to reckon as its adversary any historical vision of a universalistic order.'[12]

Mussolini praised and encouraged Evola's writings on race, which became an issue after Italy's conquest of Ethiopia in 1936. Under the influence of Nazi Germany, Italy passed Racial Laws in 1938. Evola was already writing on racial views consistent with a traditional vision of mankind in opposition to the biological reductionism and materialism of Nazi racial thought. Guido Landra, editor of the journal, *La Difesa della Razza* (Defence of the Race), was especially irritated by Evola's 1942 article, 'Scientific Racism's Mistake'. Mussolini, however, had praised Evola's article on 'Race and Culture' (translated in this volume) before the Ethiopian War.[1] He approved the translation of Evola's

---

10   A James Gregor, *Mussolini's Intellectuals: Fascist Social and Political Thought* (Princeton, NJ: Princeton University Press, 2005), p. 199.

11   The relevant passages are collected in Evola, *Cammino*, pp. 292–296.

12   Yvon de Begnac (Francesco Perfetti, ed.), *Taccuini Mussoliniani* (Bologna: Il Mulino, 1990), p. 647; *Cammino*, p. 296.

Sintesi di dottrina della razza [Summary of Racial Doctrine] into German as *Grundrisse der Faschistischen Rassenlehre* [Compendium of Fascist Racial Doctrine] to represent the official Fascist position.[13]

Evola accepts the traditional division of man into body, soul, and spirit, and argues that there are races of all three. 'While in a "pure blood" horse or cat the biological element constitutes the central one, and therefore racial considerations can be legitimately restricted to it, this is certainly not the case with man, or at least any man worthy of the name... Therefore racial treatment of man cannot stop only at a biological level.'[14] Just as the state creates the people and the nation, so spirit shapes the races of body and soul. Evola also wrote a history of racial thought, *Il mito del sangue: Genesi del razzismo* [The Blood Myth: The Genesis of Racism],[15] where he discusses the scientific racism of Gobineau, Houston Stewart Chamberlain, Alfred Rosenberg, and Landra, and the tradition of valuing extra- or super-biological elements, whose adherents included Montaigne, Herder, Fichte, Gustave Le Bon, and his friend, Ludwig Ferdinand Clauss, a German biologist at the University of Berlin.[16]

The fall of Fascism in 1943 meant the end of the initiatives of Evola and Mussolini to develop a view of race which was distinctively Fascist and rejected biological reductionism. Scientific racists dismissed Evola as a rank amateur and the average Italian remembered only that he had written books on race and so was a 'racist'. Concerning Evola's relations with Mussolini, it may be worth noting that after Mussolini was removed from power in the coup of 25 July 1943, he was handed over to partisans and was rescued from them in a daring assault led by

13   Julius Evola, *The Path of Cinnabar* , p.166; *Cammino*, p. 300.

14   *Sintesi di dottrina della razza* (Milan: Hoepli, 1941), p. 35. In the German translation (Berlin: Runge, 1943), p. 90, the last sentence reads 'Fascist racial doctrine (*die faschistischen Rassenlehre*) therefore holds a purely biological view of race to be inadequate.'

15   *Il mito del sangue: Genesi del razzismo* (Rome: Hoepli, 1937), revised 1942.

16   Ludwig Ferdinand Clauss, *Rasse und Seele: Eine Einführung in den Sinn der leiblichen Gestalt* (Munich: Lehmann, 1926, 1937); *Rasse und Charakter* (Frankfort am Main: Moritz Diesterweg, 1938).

Otto Skorzeny on 12 September 1943. Evola was one of a small group of Italians present at Hitler's headquarters at Rastenburg when Mussolini was brought there. He was disappointed when the next day Mussolini proclaimed the Italian Social Republic, although he understood it was only natural for Mussolini to turn against monarchy in response to the King's betrayal. Evola also mentioned the influence of Hitler's open contempt for monarchy.[17] Since he disapproved of the socialist and populist ideology of the Italian Social Republic, Evola did not follow Mussolini to its capital, Saló, in northern Italy. 'Nevertheless, I could not avoid acknowledging the warrior and legionary value of those hundreds of thousands of Italians who had chosen to remain loyal to their allies and to continue the war…conscious of waging a lost war, yet eager to safeguard the honour of their country. This remains an almost unique event in the history of Italy since the Roman Empire.'[18]

Many Fascists spurned Evola, but a few valued him. As the articles translated in this volume show, he was open to individuals and movements that could provide the basis for opposition to modern degeneracy and the restoration of the Golden Age. Although clear on principles, he welcomed allies even when they did not share all his own commitments, as, for instance, with his admiration for Corneliu Codreanu, the head of the Romanian Iron Guard. Codreanu had a principled commitment to tradition, the legionary spirit, and asceticism, although he was also a Christian. Codreanu evaluated the different roles of the Right-wing movements of the thirties. Fascism represented the state and form, while Nazism was based on race and nation. He saw the Iron Guard as representing spirit. Evola asked him about the role of Christianity, which Evola rejected because of its universalism. Codreanu acknowledged Evola's reservations, but explained, 'We aim to bring back to life in the form of a national consciousness

---

17   Julius Evola, *Fascism Viewed from the Right* (London: Arktos, 2013), p. 56.

18   Evola, *The Path of Cinnabar*, p. 182; *Cammino*, p. 328.

and a lived experience what in this religion has often been mummified and become the traditionalism of a somnolent clergy. [...] The Iron Guard movement takes from our religion a fundamental idea, that of *ecumenicity*. This means the overcoming of every abstract and rationalistic internationalism and universalism. The ecumenical idea is that of *societas* as a unity of life, a living organism, living together not only with our people but also with our dead and with God. [...] An important point is that for us the presence of the dead in the ecumenical nation is not abstract, but real. We cannot separate ourselves from the presence of our dead and especially our heroes. As forces liberated from the human condition they penetrate and sustain our highest life. The legionnaires meet periodically in little groups, called "nests". These meetings follow special rites. Every meeting begins with the call to all our fallen comrades and those present respond with "present!" For us this rite is not just a ceremony and allegory, but a real evocation.'

Evola refused to be discouraged by the murder of Codreanu, the fall of Mussolini, and the defeat of the Axis powers in the Second World War. The principles of a true Right remained true and valid. Even a crippling injury he suffered during an air raid in Vienna near the war's end did not stop him from meeting with young people and formulating key principles for them.

In 'Orientations,' Evola attempted to present to the post-war youth an alternative to the world they found themselves in, where the only options seemed to be the egalitarian levelling of the Communist world, the stifling consumerism represented by the United States, and the Catholic moralism of Christian Democracy. 'Orientations' remains the clearest short presentation of his principles. The Italian authorities obviously agreed, for he was soon charged with violating the recently passed laws on re-founding the Fascist Party. The police had arrested about thirty youngsters, who ranged from real but harmless rabble-rousers to more thoughtful young men who edited a Right-wing

xxii   A TRADITIONALIST CONFRONTS FASCISM

journal called *Imperium* and had arranged for the publication of 'Orientations'. Evola was arrested and tried for 'defending Fascism', 'attempting to reconstitute the dissolved Fascist Party', and being the 'master' and 'inspirer' of young neo-Fascists. Like Socrates, he was accused of not worshipping the gods of democracy and of corrupting youth.

The trial was a public relations disaster for the new democracy. A respected if somewhat rambunctious monarchist lawyer, Francesco Carnelutti, defended him free of charge. He made a mockery of the hapless prosecutors. Evola delivered his own defence speech, which was soon published. He did not disguise the fact that he had not been a typical Fascist, or even a Fascist at all. He had never joined the Fascist Party, opposed the reconciliation with the Church, mocked Fascist initiatives like the demographic campaign, and even denounced *gli squadristi*. There had been social and even physical consequences, but the government had never brought formal charges against him. That, however, had been Fascism; this was democracy. As Evola told the jury, 'Some like to depict Fascism as a "sinister tyranny". During that "tyranny" I never had to undergo a situation like the present one.'

He asked the prosecutor, Dr. Sangiorgi, where in his published writings he had defended 'distinctively Fascist ideas'. Sangiorgi admitted that there were no such specific passages, but that the general spirit of his works promoted 'Fascist ideas', such as monocracy, hierarchism, aristocracy, or elitism. Evola responded, 'I should say that if such are the terms of the accusation, I would be honoured to see seated here next to me as defendants men such as Aristotle, Plato, the Dante of *De Monarchia*, and so on, up to Metternich and Bismarck.' At this point, Evola's lawyer Carnelutti shouted out, '*La polizia è andata in cerca anche di costoro!*' ('The police have gone to look for them, too!')

Evola ignored this outburst and continued, 'In the same spirit as a Metternich, a Bismarck, or the great Catholic philosophers of the principle of authority, de Maistre and Donoso Cortés, I reject all that which derives, directly or indirectly, from the French Revolution and which, in my opinion, has as its extreme consequence Bolshevism; to which I oppose the "world of Tradition"... My principles are only those that, before the French Revolution, every well-born person considered healthy and normal.'

The jury found Evola 'innocent', a possible verdict in Roman Civil Law, which differs here from English Common Law, where the only possible verdicts are 'guilty' or 'not guilty'. The legal strategy was a good one: the Left is out to get a good conservative by calling him a Fascist. There is no reason to think the jury read 'Orientations'. If they had, they would probably have agreed that Evola's ideas are not distinctively Fascist. From the Leftist perspective they are worse. He describes the Axis as three great historic nations that had the courage to take up their traditions against the modern forces of economic reductionism, both Communist and capitalist. 'The great illusion of our days is that democracy and liberalism are the antithesis of Communism. [...] This illusion is like saying that dusk is the antithesis of night. [...] From the point of view of the idea that inspires them, Russia and North America can be considered as two tongs of the same pincers that are tightening definitively around Europe.' The true enemy is economic reductionism, or economism, which Evola calls 'hallucination or demonic possession'. The proper response to this enemy and the forces and nations that promote it is the legionary spirit, described by Evola as 'the attitude of one who knows how to choose the hardest path, to fight even when he knows that the battle is substantially lost, to confirm the words of the ancient saga, "Loyalty is stronger than fire!"' This is the ideal of Oswald Spengler's Roman soldier, who died at his post at Pompeii as the sky fell on him, because he had not been relieved.[19] Europeans do not need programs and marketing strategies, 'the skills of agitators and

---

19   Oswald Spengler, *Man and Technics: A Contribution to a Philosophy of Life* (London: Arktos, 2015), p. 77.

politicians', but men such as that. They should not worry about being on the wrong side of History. 'There is no such thing as History, this mysterious entity with a capital H. It is men, provided they are *really* men, who make and unmake history.'

Evola was not an influential figure in the Italy of the *Ventennio*, the Fascist 'Twenty Years', but his voice was heard. Today only academic experts can identify major players of the day like Giuseppe Bottai or Guido Landra. Evola's influence has grown with time. In 1951 the Italian democracy tried to send him to jail. During the years of student protest in the 1960s, Giorgio Almirante, veteran of the Italian Social Republic and President of the Italian Social Movement (MSI), called Evola 'our Marcuse, only better'. Today his works have been translated into German, French, and English, and re-edited with introductions and extensive annotation. He did what he thought was right and he wrote what he thought was true. His voice still challenges the modern world.

'The only thing that counts is this: today we find ourselves in the midst of a world in ruins. And the problem to pose is: do men still exist who are on their feet in the midst of these ruins? And what must they do, what can they still do?'

Evola's questions are still relevant. He speaks not to a globalist vision where each individual is an atomistic consumer, but to Codreanu's ecumenical ideal of *societas*. In Edmund Burke's words, 'Society is indeed a contract. [...] It is a partnership in all science; a partnership in all art; a partnership in every virtue, and in all perfection. As the ends of such a partnership cannot be obtained in many generations, it becomes a partnership not only between those who are living, but between those who are living, those who are dead, and those who are to be born.'[20] The dead have a voice in our deliberations and no small one. As T S Eliot saw, 'The communication of the dead is tongued

---

20   Edmund Burke, *Revolutionary Writings* (Cambridge: Cambridge University Press, 2014), pp. 100–101.

with fire beyond the language of the living.'[21] Julius Evola's words are tongued with fire. They give light and warmth to those still on their feet amidst the ruins.

E Christian Kopff was born in Brooklyn, New York in 1946. He completed his Bachelor's degree summa cum laude at Haverford College, and his PhD in Classics at the University of North Carolina at Chapel Hill. He is currently Associate Professor of Classics at the University of Colorado, Boulder, where he has taught since 1973. He has served as Associate Director of the University's Honors Program since 1990 and Director of its Center for Western Civilization since 2004. He also works with the University of Urbino in Italy on ancient Greek metrics and lyric poetry. He is a Fellow of the American Academy in Rome and has been awarded grants from the National Endowment for the Humanities. He is the author of *The Devil Knows Latin: Why America Needs the Classical Tradition* (ISI Books, 1999), editor of a critical edition of the Greek text of Euripides' *Bacchae* (Teubner, 1982), translator of Josef Pieper, *Tradition: Concept and Claim* (ISI Books, 2008), and has written articles and reviews on scholarly, pedagogical, and popular topics. He is also the translator of Guillaume Faye's *Convergence of Catastrophes* (2012), as well as Julius Evola's *Fascism Viewed from the Right* and *Notes on the Third Reich* (both 2013), all published by Arktos.

---

21   T S Eliot, 'Little Gidding', in *Complete Poems and Plays* (New York: Harcourt, Brace & World, 1971), p. 139.

ORIENTATIONS: ELEVEN POINTS

(1950)

Point 1.

There is no point in indulging in wishful thinking with the illusions of any kind of optimism: today we find ourselves at the end of a cycle. Already for centuries, at first insensibly, then with the momentum of a landslide, multiple processes have destroyed every normal and legitimate human order in the West and falsified every higher conception of living, acting, knowing, and fighting. And the momentum of this fall, its velocity, its giddiness, has been called 'progress'. And we have raised hymns to 'progress' and deluded ourselves that this civilisation — a civilisation of matter and machines — was civilisation *par excellence*, the one for which the entire history of the world was preordained: until the final consequences of this entire process has been such as to cause some people at least to wake up.

It is well known where and under what symbols the forces for a possible resistance tried to organise. On one side, a nation that, since it had been unified, had known nothing but the mediocre climate of liberalism, democracy, and a constitutional monarchy, dared to assume the symbol of Rome as the basis for a new political conception and a new ideal of virility and dignity. Analogous forces awoke in the nation that in the Middle Ages had made the Roman symbol of *imperium*[1] its own in order to reaffirm the principle of authority and the primacy of those values that are rooted in the blood, race, and the deepest powers of a stock. And while in other European nations, groups were already orienting themselves in the same direction, a third force in Asia joined the ranks, the nation of the *samurai*, in which the adoption of the outer forms of modern civilisation had not prejudiced its fidelity to a warrior tradition centred upon the symbol of the solar empire of divine right.

No one claims that there was a very clear discrimination between the essential and the accessory in these currents, that in them the idea was confronted by people of high quality who understood it, or that various influences arising from the very forces that had to be combatted had been overcome. The process of ideological purification would have taken place at a later time, once some immediate and unavoidable political problems had been resolved. But even so it was clear that a marshalling of forces was taking shape, representing an open challenge to 'modern' civilisation: both to those democracies that are the heirs of the French Revolution, and to the other one, which represents the extreme limit of the degradation of Western man: the collectivistic civilisation of the Fourth Estate,[2] the Communist civilisation of the faceless mass-man. Rhythms accelerated, and tensions increased until the opposing forces met in armed combat. What prevailed was the massive power of a coalition that did not draw back from the most hybridised of agreements and the most hypocritical ideological mobilisation in order to crush the world that was raising itself and intended to affirm its right. Whether or not our men were equal to the task, whether errors were committed in matters of timing, preparation,

---

1   *Imperium* designated the authority of the Roman state to rule over its individual subjects.—Ed.

2   In *Men Among the Ruins*, Evola defines the Fourth Estate as being the last stage in the cyclical development of the social elite, beginning with the monarchy; in the final phase of history, he says, 'the fourth and last elite is that of the collectivist and revolutionary leaders of the Fourth Estate' (p. 164).—Ed.

or the assessment of risks, let us leave that aside, because it does not prejudice the internal significance of the struggle that was fought. Equally, it does not interest us that today history is taking its revenge on the victors; that the democratic powers, after allying themselves with the forces of red subversion to conduct the war all the way to the senseless extremism of unconditional surrender and total destruction, today see their allies of yesterday turn on them as a danger much more frightening than the one they wanted to exorcise.

The only thing that counts is this: today we find ourselves in the midst of a world in ruins. The problem to pose is, do men on their feet still exist in the midst of these ruins? And what must they do, what can they still do?

Point 2.

Such a problem, in truth, goes far beyond yesterday's coalitions, because it is clear that both victors and defeated now find themselves on the same level, and the only result of the Second World War has been to reduce Europe to the object of extra-European powers and interests. We have to recognise that the devastation we have around us is primarily of a moral character. We are in a climate of general moral amnesia and of profound disorientation, despite all the accepted ways of speaking in common use in a society of consumers and democracy: the surrender of character and every true dignity, an ideological wasting away, the supremacy of the lowest interests, and living day by day, in general characterise post-war man. Recognising this means also recognising that the first problem, the foundation of every other one, is of an internal character: getting up on your feet, standing up inside, giving oneself a form, and creating in oneself an order and uprightness. People who delude themselves today about the possibility of a purely political struggle and about the power of one or another formula or system, who do not possess a new human quality as a precise opposing vision, have learned none of the lessons of the recent past. Here is a principle that ought to be absolutely clear today more than ever: if a state were to possess a political or social system that, in theory, would count as the most perfect one, but the human substance of which it is comprised were tainted, well then, that state would sooner or later descend to the level of the lowest societies, while a people, a race capable of producing real men, men of just feeling and secure instinct, would reach a high level of civilisation and would stay on its feet before the most calamitous tests even if its political system were faulty and imperfect. We should therefore take a firm stand against that false "political realism" that thinks only in terms of programmes, partisan political issues, and social and economic recipes. All this belongs to the contingent, not the essential. The measure of what can still be saved rather depends on the existence, or absence, of men who stand before us not to recite talking points, but to be models: not yielding to the demagogy or materialism of the masses, but to revive different forms of sensibilities and interests. Beginning with what can still survive among the ruins, and slowly to construct a new man to be animated by means of a determined spirit and an adequate vision of life, and fortified by means of an iron adherence to given principles — this is the real problem.

Point 3.

As spirit there exists something that can serve as an outline for the forces of resistance and revival: it is the *legionary spirit*. It is the attitude of one who knows how to choose the hardest life, to fight even when he knows that the battle is substantially lost, and to confirm the words of the ancient saga: 'Loyalty is stronger than fire.' Through him the traditional idea is affirmed. It is the sense of honour and shame — not half-hearted measures drawn from half-hearted morals — that creates a substantial difference, an existential difference between beings, almost as though between one race and another race.

On the other hand, there is the realisation that belongs to those in whom what was an end now appears as only a means. They recognise the illusory character of manifold myths, while leaving intact what they know how to follow *for themselves*, on the frontiers between life and death, beyond the world of the contingent.

These forms of spirit can be the foundation of a new unity. What is essential is to seize them, apply them, and extend them from wartime to peacetime, especially this peace that is only a moment of respite and a poorly controlled disorder — until distinctions and a new grouping are established. This has to happen in rather more essential terms than what might be called a 'party', which can only be a contingent instrument in view of given political struggles; in terms more essential even than a simple 'movement', if by 'movement' we understand only a phenomenon of masses and aggregation, a quantitative phenomenon more than a qualitative one, based more on emotional factors than on severe, clear adherence to an idea. What we are hoping for, rather, is a silent revolution, proceeding in the depths, in which the premises are created, first internally and in individuals, of that Order that will later have to affirm itself externally as well, supplanting suddenly, at the right moment, the forms and forces of a world of subversion. The 'style' that has to achieve prominence is that of one who holds his positions out of loyalty to himself and to an idea, in an intense absorption, in a rejection of every compromise, in a total commitment that must manifest itself not only in the political struggle, but also in every expression of existence: factories, laboratories, universities, the streets, and the very personal life of the affections. We need to reach the point where the type of which we speak, which must be the cellular substance of our group, is completely recognisable, unmistakable, and differentiated. Then we can say, 'He is one who acts like a man of the movement.'

This was the commitment of the forces which dreamed of a new order for Europe, but which was often frustrated and misled in realising it by manifold factors. Today that commitment must be taken up again. And today, the conditions are basically better, because the situation has become clearer. We only need to look around, from the public squares all the way to Parliament, to see that our vocations are being tested, and that we have clearly in front of us the measure of what we should not be. Before a world of mush, whose principles are, 'You have no choice', or else, 'We'll have time for morals after we take care of our stomach and our skin.' (I mean 'skin' in the sense of Curzio Malaparte's novel, *The Skin*!)[3] There is also, 'These are not times in which we can permit ourselves the luxury of having character.' Or last and least, 'I have a family.' When we hear these slogans, we know how to give a clear and firm response: 'As for us, we cannot act in any other way. This is our life, this is our essence.' Whatever positive achievements are accomplished today or tomorrow, it will not be by means of the skills of agitators and political operatives, but by the natural prestige and recognition of men both of yesterday and, even more, of the new generation, who are capable of so much and thus vouch for their idea.

Point 4.

Therefore there is a new substance that must make its way in a slow advance beyond the boxes, columns, and social positions of the past. We need to have a new figure before our eyes to measure our own force and our own vocation. It is important, or rather basic, to recognise that

---

3   Curzio Malaparte (1898–1957) was an avant-garde Italian writer and journalist. Originally a Fascist supporter, he turned against Fascism after covering the war on the Eastern Front for the Italian newspapers. In his 1949 novel *The Skin*, the book's narrator says, 'Our skin, this confounded skin. You've no idea what a man will do, what deeds of heroism and infamy he can accomplish, to save his skin' (*The Skin* [New York: New York Review of Books, 2013]).—Ed.

this figure has nothing to do with classes as economic categories and with the antagonisms related to them. This figure can present itself in the garb of rich as well as poor, of worker as well as aristocrat, of businessman as well as explorer, technician, theologian, farmer, and even a politician in the strict sense. But this new substance will know an internal differentiation, which will be complete when, again, there will be no doubts about the vocations and functions to follow and command; when a repristinated symbol of unshaken authority will reign at the centre of new hierarchical structures.

This formulation defines a direction that calls itself as much anti-bourgeois as anti-proletarian, a direction completely liberated from democratic contaminations and 'social' whims, because it leads to a world that is clear, virile, articulated, and made of men and men's guides. It has contempt for the bourgeois myth of 'security', and the petty life that is standardised, conformist, domesticated, and 'moral-ised'. Contempt for the anodyne fetter that is part and parcel of every collectivist and mechanical system and all the ideologies that attribute to confused 'social' values the primacy over those heroic and spiritual values with which the true man, the absolute person, ought to be de-fined for us in *every* area. Something essential will have been achieved when we revive the love for a style of active impersonality, through which what counts is the work and not the individual. Through this, we become capable of not seeing ourselves as something important, since what is important is the function, the responsibility, the task accepted, and the end pursued. Where this spirit is achieved, many problems will be simplified, including problems of economic and social order, which would otherwise remain insoluble if confronted from outside, without the counterpart of a change of spiritual factors and without the elimination of ideological infections that from the beginning, already hinder every return to the normal; in fact, even the very perception of what normal means.

Point 5.

It is important not only for doctrinal orientation, but also in regard to the world of action, that the men of the new group precisely recognise the chain of causes and effects and the essential continuity of the current that has given life to the various political forms that are jousting today in the chaos of the parties. Liberalism, then democracy, then socialism, then radicalism, and finally Communism and Bolshevism, only appeared historically as steps taken by the same evil, as stages in which each one prepares the next in the complex unity of a process of decline. The beginning of this process is the point at which Western man shattered the fetters of tradition, rejected every superior symbol of authority and sovereignty, claimed a vain and illusory liberty for himself as an individual, and became an atom instead of a conscious part in the organic and hierarchical unity of a whole. In the end, the atom was bound to find that the mass of the other atoms, the other individuals, had turned against him, and he was dragged into the plight of the kingdom of quantity, of pure number, of masses that are given over completely to materialism and who have no other god than the sovereign economy. In this process there is no stopping halfway down the road. Without the French Revolution and liberalism, there would not have been constitutionalism and democracy; without democracy there would not have been socialism and demagogic nationalism; without the preparation of socialism there would not have been radicalism and, finally, Communism. The fact that today we see these different forms frequently together or in opposition should not prevent an eye that sees clearly from recognising that they belong together. They are linked, they condition one another in turn, and they express only the different steps of the same current, the same subversion of every normal and legitimate social ordering. The great illusion of our days is that democracy and liberalism are the antithesis of Communism and have the power to stem the tide of the forces of the low, what is called the 'progressive' movement in the jargon of the labour unions. This illusion is like saying that dusk is the antithesis of night, that an illness's incipient stage is the antithesis of its acute and endemic stage, or that a diluted poison is the antithesis of the same poison in its pure and concentrated state. The men in the government of this 'liberated' Italy have learned nothing from the recent past, although its lessons are repeated everywhere monotonously. They continue their pitiful game with political conceptions that are out of date and empty in the parliamentary Mardi Gras, this *danse macabre* on a dormant volcano. What is in our possession is the courage of radicalism, the No spoken to political decadence in all its forms, both of the Left and of the supposed Right. And we must be especially aware of this: that there is no negotiating with subversion, and that concessions made today mean condemning ourselves to being completely overwhelmed tomorrow. We therefore insist on intransigence of the idea, and a readiness to advance with pure forces, when the right moment arrives.

Naturally this also implies ridding ourselves of ideological distortion, which unfortunately is widespread even in some of our young people. It is because of this that they concede some of the excuses for the destructions that have already taken place, deluding themselves with thinking that, after all, they were necessary and will serve the cause of 'progress': that we should be fighting for something 'new', awaiting us in a definite future, instead of for truths that we already possess. This is because, always and everywhere, although these truths appear in different forms, they have been the foundation for every correct type of social and political organisation. Young people need to reject these fads and whims. We should learn to laugh at people who call us 'on the wrong side of history' and 'reactionaries'. There is no such thing as History, this mysterious entity with a capital H. Men make and unmake history, provided they are *really* men. What is called the course of history is more or less the same thing as what is called 'progressivism' in Left-wing circles, and it aims at only one thing today: to foment passivity in the face of the current that is getting stronger and carries us continually lower. As to the charge of 'reactionary', ask them the following question: while you are acting, destroying, and profaning, do you then want us not to 'react', but to stand by passively watching, or maybe even shouting, 'Good work, keep it up!' We are not 'reactionaries' only because the word is not strong enough, and especially because *we* start from what is positive, and we represent what is positive — values that are real and original, and we do not need the light of any 'sun of the future'.

In the face of our radicalism, in particular, the antithesis between red 'East' and democratic 'West' appears irrelevant. An eventual armed conflict between these two blocs appears to us even more tragically irrelevant. If we look only at the immediate future, the choice of the lesser evil is certainly a reality because the military victory of the 'East' would imply the immediate physical destruction of the last representatives of the resistance. But from the point of view of the idea that inspires them, Russia and North America can be considered as two tongs of the same pincers which are tightening inexorably around Europe. In them we see the same foreign and hostile force, acting in different but converging forms. The forms of standardisation, conformism, democratic levelling, frantic overproduction, the more or less arrogant and explicit cult of the expert ('brain trust'), and the petty materialism of Americanism can only clear the road for the final phase, which is represented in the same direction by the Communist ideal of the mass man. The distinctive trait of Americanism is that the attack on quality and personality is not accomplished by means of the brutal coercion of a Marxist dictatorship and the care of the state, but takes place almost spontaneously, by means of a civilisation that does not recognise ideals higher than wealth, consumption, profit, and unchecked economic growth — an exaggeration and *reductio ad absurdum* of what Europe herself has chosen. This is what the same motives have created there or are in the process of creating. On both sides we see the same primitivism, mechanical reductionism, and brutality. In a certain sense Americanism is for us more dangerous than Communism, because it is essentially a kind of Trojan horse. When the attack against those values of the European tradition which yet survive are found in the direct and naked form that belongs to the Bolshevik ideology and Stalinism, it still provokes some reactions and certain lines of resistance, even if weak ones, can be maintained. Things are different when the same evil acts in a subtler manner and the transformations take place insensibly on the level of custom and a general worldview, as is the case with Americanism. By thoughtlessly submitting to the influence of Americanism under the flag of democracy, Europe is already predisposed to the ultimate abdication, and this could come about without the need for a military catastrophe, but more or less the same point could be reached in a 'progressive' fashion after a final social crisis. Again, there is no stopping halfway down the slope. Americanism, willy-nilly, is working for its ostensible enemy: collectivism.

Point 6.

Our commitment to a radical reconstruction is directly relevant here because it insists there can be no dealings not only with every variety of Marxist and socialist ideology, but likewise with what in general can be called the *hallucination,* or the *demonic possession* by the economy. We are dealing here with the idea that in both the individual and collective life, the economic factor is the important, real, and decisive one; that the concentration of every value and interest upon the field of economics and production is not the unprecedented aberration of modern Western man, but on the contrary something normal; not something that is, possibly, an ugly necessity, but rather something that should be desired and exalted. Both capitalism and Marxism are trapped in this closed and dark circle. We need to break this circle wide open. As long as we talk about nothing else but economic classes, work, wages, and production; and as long as we delude ourselves that real human progress and the genuine elevation of the individual is conditioned by a particular system of distribution of wealth and goods, and therefore has to do with poverty and ease, with the state of prosperity *à la* the United States or with that of utopian socialism, we yet remain on the same level as that which we need to combat. We need to assert the following: that everything that relates to economy and the view of economic interest as a mere satisfaction of physical needs has had, has now, and always will have a subordinate role in a normal humanity. Beyond this sphere we need to separate an order of superior values which are political, spiritual, and heroic; an order that — as we already said — does not recognise, or even admit, 'proletarians' or 'capitalists'. It is only in terms of this order that it is proper to define the things for which it is worth living and dying, which establish a true hierarchy, which differentiate new ranks of dignity, and, at the top, place on the throne a superior function of command, an *Imperium*.

In light of this, we need to eradicate many weeds that have taken root here and there, sometimes even in our own field. What, after all, is this chatter regarding a 'state of labour',[4] of 'national socialism', of the 'humanism of work', and similar expressions? What are these more or less openly proclaimed appeals for an involution of politics into the economy, as if in a renewal of those problematic tendencies toward 'integral corporatism', that was basically headless, but which in Fascism fortunately found its way barred? Why do we see the slogan of 'socialisation' considered as a type of universal cure-all and the

---

4   The Fascists sometimes referred to their regime as the 'state of labour', implying that it was primarily a workers' state. This became an even greater ideal in the post-Fascist Republic of Italy.—Ed.

elevation of the 'social idea' to a symbol of a new civilisation that, who knows how, is supposed to be beyond 'East' and 'West'?

These slogans — we need to acknowledge it — are the dark sides present in quite a few minds that admittedly are in other respects found on our side. With this way of talking they think that they are being faithful to a 'revolutionary' commitment, while they are only obeying suggestions stronger than they are. A degraded political environment is full of them. Among these suggestions, the 'social question' re-enters. When will they finally realise the truth? Marxism did not arise because of the existence of a real social question, but the social question arises — in countless cases — only because Marxism exists, in other words artificially, or in terms that are almost always unsolvable, because of agitators, who are notorious for 'raising class consciousness'. Lenin expressed himself very clearly about them, when he refuted the spontaneous character of revolutionary proletarian movements.[5]

It is starting with this premise that we should act, above all, in the direction of ideological *de-proletarianisation*, by disinfecting those parts of the people which are still healthy of the socialist *virus*. Only then can one or another reform be studied and implemented without danger, according to true justice.

Thus, as a particular case, we can examine in what spirit the corporative[6] idea can again be one of the foundations of reconstruction. I mean corporatism not so much as the state's general system of composition, an almost bureaucratic system that maintains the deleterious idea of classes arrayed against one another, but rather as the demand that we must reconstruct within each business that unity and solidarity of differentiated forces which have been prejudiced and shattered, on the

---

5   Lenin devotes the second chapter of his book *What is to be Done?* to a refutation of this notion.—Ed.

6   Present-day readers may be tempted to think of the term 'corporative' and 'corporation' as something relating to companies or business ventures. Evola, however, uses the term, as did the Fascists themselves, to describe a type of society in which its citizens are organised into groups based on the function they perform for the body of the entire society itself, such as agriculture, the military, or administration.—Ed.

one hand, by capitalist prevarication (which has been followed by the parasitic type of the speculator and finance capitalist), and by Marxist agitation on the other. We must bring business into the form of an almost military unity, in which the spirit of responsibility, energy, and competence of the man who directs it will bring about the solidarity and loyalty of the working forces associated around him in a common enterprise. The only true task is, therefore, the *organic reconstruction of business*. To do this there is no need for slogans intended to be fawned upon or for low propagandistic and electoral ends, which represent the spirit of sedition of the lowest strata of the masses, a spirit which is disguised as 'social justice'. In general, we should restore the style of active impersonality, dignity, and solidarity in producing a style that belonged to the ancient corporations of artisans and professionals. We need to outlaw the trade union movement with its 'struggle' and its acts of real blackmail, of which we meet too many examples today. But, let us say again, we need to reach this point by starting from the inside. The important point is that against every form of *ressentiment*[7] and social antagonism everyone should recognise and love his own station, one that fits his own nature, also recognising in this way the limits within which he can develop his own possibilities and achieve his own perfection, because an artisan that acquits himself perfectly in his function is without doubt superior to a king that rejects and does not live up to his dignity.

In particular, we can allow a system of technical competences[8] and corporative representations to replace the partisan parliamentary system, but we should keep in mind that the technical hierarchies, on the whole, can signify only a step in the integral hierarchy. They concern the order of means, to be subordinated to the order of ends,

---

7   *Ressentiment*, literally 'resentment' from French, suggests the endless repetition of the disgust that one feels towards a person or thing, resulting in a deep-seated aversion that becomes part of a person's essential nature.—Ed.

8   'Competences' here refers to specialised areas of professional knowledge.—Ed.

to which alone corresponds the really political and spiritual part of the state. Speaking instead of a 'state of labour' or of production is the same as making a whole of the part, as clinging to what amounts to a human organism reduced to its merely physical and vital functions. Our standard can be neither such an obtuse and dark thing nor the 'social' idea. The true antithesis in front of 'East' as well as 'West' is not the 'social ideal'. It is instead the *integral hierarchical idea*. Confronted with that, no uncertainty is acceptable.

Point 7.

If the ideal of a virile and organic political unity was already an essential part of the world that was overwhelmed — and through it in Italy the Roman symbol was also recalled — we should also recognise the cases in which such a demand took the wrong path and was nearly aborted in the mistaken direction of '*totalitarianism*'. This, again, is a point that must be seen clearly, so that the two sides are precisely distinguished and, also, so that we do not furnish arms to those who want to confuse matters for reasons we have seen. Hierarchy is not hierarchism. (The latter is an evil that unfortunately tries to spring up in a minor key every once in a while.) The organic conception has nothing to do with a state-worshipping sclerosis and a levelling centralisation. As for individuals, both individualism and collectivism are really overcome only when men stand in front of men, in the natural diversity of their being and their dignity. And as for the unity that ought to, in general, impede every form of dissociation and absolutising of the particular, the unity must be essentially spiritual and of a central orienting influence; an impulse that, depending on the realms, assumes very differentiated forms of expression. This is the true essence of the 'organic' conception, which is opposed to rigid and extrinsic relations appropriate to 'totalitarianism'. In this framework the demand for the dignity and liberty of the human person, which liberalism knows how to conceive only in terms that are individualistic, egalitarian, and privatised, can be realised integrally. It is in this spirit that the structures of a new political and social order must be studied, in solid and clear articulations.

But these kinds of structures need a centre, a highest point of reference. A new symbol of sovereignty and authority is necessary. The commitment, in this regard, must be precise. Ideological tergiversations cannot be permitted. It is important to say clearly that we are dealing here only secondarily with the so-called institutional problem. We are dealing especially with what is necessary for a specific *climate*, for the fluency that ought to animate every relationship of loyalty, dedication, service, and action with no thought of individual glory, so that we have really overcome the grey, mechanical, and devious aspect of the present political and social world. Given the situation today it will end in an impasse, since at the top it is not capable of any kind of asceticism of the pure idea. The clear perception of the right direction is compromised for many, either by some unfortunate antecedents of our national traditions or, and even more so, by the tragic accidents of yesterday. We can also recognise the inconclusiveness of the monarchical solution, since we can see those people who today only know how to defend the remnant of an idea, a symbol that has been gutted and castrated, like the constitutional parliamentary monarchy. But in an equally decisive fashion we ought to proclaim the incompatibility of our idea with the republican idea. To be anti-democratic, on one hand, and to defend the republican idea 'ferociously' (this is unfortunately the terminology of some representatives of a false intransigence) on the other, is an absurdity that is almost palpable. By republic we mean modern republics. The ancient republics were aristocracies — as in Rome — or oligarchies, these latter often possessing the character of tyrannies. Modern republics belong essentially to the world that came into existence through Jacobinism and the anti-traditional and anti-hierarchical subversion of the nineteenth century. This kind of world, which is not ours, must be left behind. In terms of principle, a nation that is already monarchical and then becomes a republic can only be considered a 'downgraded' nation. In Italy we should not play a mistaken game in the name of loyalty to the Fascism of the Salò Republic,[9] because if, for that reason, we feel we ought to follow the false road of republicanism, we would at the same time be disloyal to something larger and better, and throw overboard the central nucleus of the ideology of the Twenty Years of Fascism, which is its doctrine of the state, in the function of authority, power, *imperium*.

This doctrine alone must be maintained, without agreeing to descend to a lower level or play any group's game. The concrete form of the symbol can for the present be left undecided. The essential task is to prepare in silence the suitable spiritual environment so that the symbol of a superior, untouchable authority may be felt and acquire its full significance once again, to which there cannot correspond the stature of any 'president' of a republic who can be voted out of office. Neither will the stature of a tribune or a people's leader be equal to the task, being the holder of a simple, formless individual power that is deprived of every higher chrism[10] and rests instead on the precarious prestige exercised by him over the irrational forces of the masses. It has been given the name 'Bonapartism'[11] and its significance is correctly recognised not as the antithesis of demagogic and 'popular' democracy, but instead as its logical conclusion: one of the dark apparitions

---

9   The Salò Republic, or more formally the Italian Social Republic, was the government of Fascist exiles which was set up in northern Italy, with German military support, following the occupation of the south by the Allies. Once Mussolini was instated as its head of state in September 1943, Mussolini returned to his socialist roots, and said that he had been prevented from realising the genuine Fascist revolution by political contingencies, and pledged to create a new Fascist state that was much more republican and socialist in nature.—Ed.

10   A type of anointing oil used in many branches of Christianity.—Ed.

11   Bonapartism refers to a circumstance where the ideals of a political revolution are co-opted by a dictator who uses it to further his own power aims, as Napoleon did with the French Revolution.—Ed.

of Spengler's 'decline of the West'.[12] This is a new touchstone for our side: a *sensibility* in respect to all this. Carlyle[13] has already talked of the 'Valet-World', who *has* to be governed by the Sham-Hero',[14] not a real Lord.

Point 8.

We must clarify another point in an analogous order of ideas. We are talking about the position to take in response to nationalism and the general idea of fatherland. This discussion is all the more relevant, because today many, trying to salvage what can be saved, would like to take up a sentimental and, at the same time, naturalistic conception of the nation. This notion is foreign to the highest European political tradition and is difficult to reconcile with the idea of the state that we have already discussed. Even leaving to one side the fact that we see the idea of fatherland invoked by the most divergent parties, even by representatives of red subversion, this conception is already in fact not relevant to the times, because, on one hand, we are witnessing the creation of large, supranational blocs, while, on the other, the necessity of finding a European reference point is increasingly apparent, a unifying one beyond the inevitable particularism inherent in the naturalistic idea of the nation and still more of 'nationalism'. Still, the question of principle is more essential. The political level *per se* is one of superior unities when compared to unities defined in naturalistic terms like those to which the general notions of nation, fatherland, and people

---

12 This refers to the book *The Decline of the West* (New York: Knopf, 1926/28), in which Spengler theorised that all civilisations go through an inevitable cycle of ages of rise and decline in power, with the present age, which has been dominated by the West, currently entering its declining period. Spengler's thesis bears some similarity to traditional doctrines, but, as Spengler was a Nietzschean, he did not view his theoretical cycle as being the result of a transcendent, metaphysical reality.—Ed.

13 Thomas Carlyle (1795–1881) was a Scottish writer who was extremely influential in the nineteenth century. His book, *On Heroes, Hero-Worship, and The Heroic in History* (1841), portrays human history as being driven by extraordinary individuals.—Ed.

14 Thomas Carlyle, *On Heroes, Hero-Worship, and the Heroic in History* (London: James Fraser, 1841), p. 350.—Ed.

correspond. On this superior level, what unites and what divides is the idea: an idea borne by a definite elite and tending to achieve concrete form in the state. For this Fascist doctrine — that in this aspect remained faithful to the best European political tradition — gave first place to idea and state as compared to nation and people, and understood that nation and people acquire a significance and a form, and participate in a higher grade of existence, only within the state. It is precisely in periods of crisis, like the present, that it is necessary to hold firmly to this doctrine. Our true fatherland must be recognised in the idea. What counts is not coming from the same land or speaking the same language, but sharing the same idea. This is the foundation and the starting point. To the collectivistic unity of the nation — *des enfants de la patrie*[15] — such as has increasingly dominated ever since the Jacobin revolution,[16] we oppose something like an Order in every situation: men loyal to principles, witnesses of a higher authority and legitimacy that proceed precisely from the idea. As for practical goals, today we can hope to reach a new national solidarity, but to reach it we must not descend to compromises. The presupposition, without which every success would be illusory, is separating and forming a grouping defined by the idea — as political idea and vision of life. There is no other way, especially today. In the midst of ruins we must renew the process of originating; one that, in terms of elites and a symbol of sovereignty and authority, makes a people become one among the traditional great states, like forms rising out of the formless. Not understanding this realism of the idea means remaining on a level that is fundamentally sub-political, that of naturalism and sentimentalism, if not of downright chauvinistic rhetoric.

15 French for 'the children of the Fatherland', the phrase occurs in the first line of *La Marseillaise*, the national anthem of France since the French Revolution.—Ed.

16 The Jacobin Club, a political group in eighteenth-century France, was one of the driving forces of the French Revolution.—Ed.

We must be especially attentive where there is a desire to use national traditions to support our idea, because a complete 'national history' of Masonic and anti-traditional inspiration exists that specialises in attributing the Italian national character to the most problematic aspects of our history, beginning with the revolt of the communes with the support of Guelphism.[17] This historical vision emphasises a tendentious 'Italian character', in which we cannot and do not wish to recognise ourselves, and which we happily leave to those Italians who, with the 'Liberation' and the partisan movement,[18] have celebrated a 'second *Risorgimento*'.[19]

Idea, order, elite, state, men of the Order — we should maintain the battle lines in these terms, for as long as possible.

Point 9.

Something must be said regarding the problem of culture. Not too much, however. In fact, we do not overvalue culture. What we call 'worldview' is not based on books. It is rather an internal form that can be clearer in a person without a particular culture than in an 'intellectual' or a writer. We should attribute to the evil consequences of a 'free culture' that is within everyone's reach the fact that the individual is left open to influences of every sort, even when he is the sort of person who cannot be actively engaged with them or know how to discriminate and judge correctly.

---

17   Guelph is a thirteenth-century term which was originally coined to name the supporters of the Pope, who were in conflict with the Ghibellines, who supported the imperial power of the Hohenstaufen throne against Papal authority. Evola saw this conflict as highlighting the distinction between priestly and royal authority in the state, since he believed the Ghibelline view to be the only valid one from a traditional perspective. He discusses this at length in *Revolt Against the Modern World* and *The Mystery of the Grail*. The communes were city-states which retained a degree of independence from their rulers in the Holy Roman Empire. In the 1240s, some of the communes sided with the Guelphs against the Emperor.—Ed.

18   The Liberation refers to the end of Fascist rule, and the partisans were those who fought against the Fascists in northern Italy between 1943 and 1945, many of whom were of a Communist orientation.—Ed.

19   The *Risorgimento* ('resurgence') refers to the conquest and unification of the various states on the Italian peninsula by the House of Savoy, the rulers of Piedmont in northern Italy.—Ed.

This is not the right place to discuss this issue except to point out that, as things stand nowadays, there are specific currents against which today's youth ought to defend itself internally. We have talked first of a style of uprightness and self-possession. This style implies a just knowledge, and young people in particular should recognise the poison which has been given to an entire generation by the concordant varieties of a distorted and false vision of life that has affected their inner forces. In one form or another, these poisons continue to act in culture, science, sociology, and literature, like so many hotbeds of infection that must be identified and attacked. Apart from historical materialism and economism, of which we have already spoken, among the most important of these are Darwinism, psychoanalysis, and existentialism.

Against Darwinism we must reclaim the fundamental dignity of the human person by recognising its true place, which is not that of an individual, more or less evolved animal species among so many others, differentiated by 'natural selection' and always linked to bestial and primitivistic origins. Rather it is one which can be elevated virtually beyond the biological level. Even if there is less talk of Darwinism today, its substance remains. The biologistic Darwinian myth, in one variant or another, has the precise value of dogma, defended by the anathemas of 'science', in the materialism of both Marxist and American civilisation. Modern man has gotten used to this degraded conception, tranquilly recognising himself in it and finding it natural.

Against psychoanalysis we should oppose the ideal of an ego which does not abdicate, and which intends to remain conscious, autonomous, and sovereign in the face of the nocturnal and subterranean part of his soul and the demonic character of sexuality. This ego does not feel either 'repressed' or psychotically torn apart, but achieves an equilibrium of all his faculties ordered in accordance with a higher significance of living and acting. An obvious convergence can be noted:

authority has been stripped from the conscious principle of the person and the subconscious, the irrational, the 'collective unconscious', and similar ideas from psychoanalysis and analogous schools have been given prominence in its place. In the individual, these correspond exactly to what in the modern social and historical world is represented by the crisis, the movement from below, subversion, the revolutionary substitution of the higher by the lower, and the contempt for every principle of authority present in the modern social and historical world. The same tendency is acting on two different levels and the two effects must end up becoming united in turn.

As for existentialism, even if we distinguish what is properly a philosophy — a confused philosophy — that up until yesterday remained relevant only to narrow circles of specialists, it is necessary to recognise in it the spiritual state of a crisis that has become systematised and fawned upon, being the truth of a shattered and contradictory human type which experiences a liberty by which it does not feel elevated as anguish, tragic fate, and absurdity. Such people feel rather condemned without escape and responsibility to this end in the midst of a world stripped of value and meaning. All this, when the best of Nietzsche had already indicated a way to rediscover a sense of existence and to give oneself a law and a value untouchable even in the face of a radical nihilism, under the banner of a *positive* existentialism, according to his own expression: that of a 'noble nature'.

Such are the lines of overcoming, which should not be intellectualistic, but lived and realised in their direct significance for the inner life and its own conduct. Getting back on our feet is not possible as long as we remain in any way under the influence of similar forms of a false and twisted way of thinking. Only when you have freed yourself from dependence on drugs can you attain clarity, uprightness, and force.

Point 10.

In the zone that stands between culture and custom it will be a good idea to explain the proper attitude more clearly. From Communism was launched the standing order of the anti-bourgeois attitude that has also been picked up by the field of culture in certain 'committed' intellectual environments. This is a point which we need to see very clearly. Just as bourgeois society is something intermediate, so there are two possible ways to overcome the bourgeoisie, to say No to the bourgeois type, bourgeois civilisation, and the bourgeois spirit and its values. One possibility corresponds to the direction that leads on to the lowest point of all this, towards a collectivistic and materialised humanity with its 'realism' in the Marxist style: social and proletarian values against 'bourgeois and capitalist decadence'. The other possibility is the direction that combats the bourgeoisie in order to effectively raise oneself beyond it. The men of the new grouping will be, yes, anti-bourgeois, but by means of the aforementioned superior, heroic, and aristocratic conception of existence. They will be anti-bourgeois because they despise the easy life; anti-bourgeois because they will follow not those who promise material advantages, but those who demand all of themselves; anti-bourgeois, finally, because they are not preoccupied with security but love an essential union between life and risk, on all levels, making their own the inexorable character of the naked idea and the precise action. Yet another aspect by which the new man, the basic cell for the movement of reawakening, will be anti-bourgeois and will differentiate himself from the previous generation, is by his intolerance for every form of rhetoric and false idealism, for all those big words that are written with capital letters; for everything that is only gesture, phrase, effect, and scenery. The essential, on the other hand, is a new realism in measuring oneself exactly by the problems that will face us, and in acting so that what counts is not appearance, but being; not gossiping, but accomplishing, in a silent and exact manner, in harmony with related forces and adhering to the command that comes from above.

Whoever knows how to react against the forces of the Left only in the name of idols, the lifestyle, and the mediocre, conformist morality of the bourgeois world, has already lost the battle beforehand. This is not the case for the man who stands on his feet, having already passed through the purifying fire of outer and inner destruction. Just as this man politically is not the instrument of a bourgeois pseudo-reaction, so, in general, he restores forces and ideals older than and superior to the bourgeois world and the economic era. With these forces and ideals he creates the lines of defence and consolidates the positions from whence, at the right moment, the action of reconstruction will blaze forth.

In regard to this, we also intend to restore a commitment that was not achieved, because we know that there was an anti-bourgeois tendency during the Fascist period that wanted to express itself in a similar direction. Unfortunately, here too the human substance was not equal to the task, and it was possible to make rhetoric even from the steadfast rejection of rhetoric.

Point 11.

Let us briefly consider a last point: relations with the dominant religion. For us, the secular state, in whatever form, belongs to the past. In particular, we oppose that travesty that has become known in certain circles as the 'ethical state',[20] the product of a broken-winded, spurious,

---

20   The Fascist state made attempts to instil morality in the Italians, particularly in the area of sexual mores; in *Fascism Viewed from the Right*, Evola condemns such efforts as belonging to 'little morality' and of being bourgeois in character.—Ed.

empty 'Idealist' philosophy that attached itself to Fascism,[21] but by its nature was able to give equal support, by the simple device of a 'dialectical' game of dice, to Croce's[22] anti-Fascism.

But if we oppose similar ideologies and the secular state, for us a clerical and clericalising state is equally unacceptable. A religious factor is necessary as a background for a truly heroic conception of life, such as must be essential for our group. It is necessary to feel the evidence in ourselves that beyond this earthly life there is a higher life, because only someone who feels this way possesses a force that cannot be broken or overwhelmed. Only this kind of person will be capable of an absolute leap. When this feeling is lacking, challenging death and placing no value on his own life is possible only in sporadic moments of exaltation and in an unleashing of irrational forces; nor is there a discipline that can justify itself with a higher and autonomous significance in such an individual. But this spirituality, which ought to be alive among our people, does not need the obligatory dogmatic formulations of a given religious confession. The lifestyle that must be led is not that of Catholic moralism, which aims at little more than a domestication of the human animal based on virtue. Politically, this spirituality can only nourish diffidence before everything that is an integral part of the Christian conception, like humanitarianism, equality, the principle of love, and forgiveness, instead of honour and justice. Certainly, if Catholicism were capable of making a capacity for high asceticism its own, and precisely on that basis to make of the faith the soul of an armed bloc of forces, almost like a resumption of the spirit of the best aspects of the Middle Ages of the Crusades — almost a new

21 Evola is referring to Giovanni Gentile (1875–1944), who was Italy's leading philosopher in the Idealist tradition. He was among the most important theoreticians and intellectual spokesmen of Fascism. His ideas contributed to the idea of the 'ethical state'. Idealism comprises many different schools of thought, but its basic premise is that reality as we perceive it is concocted in our minds, and is a product of thought, rather than something that is objectively real.—Ed.

22 Benedetto Croce (1866–1952) was a highly influential Italian art critic, senator, and a philosopher in the German Idealist tradition. He initially supported Italian Fascism, but by 1925 he had become an opponent of the regime.—Ed.

order of Templars that will be compact and inexorable against the currents of chaos, surrender, subversion, and the practical materialism of the modern world — in a case like this, and even if at minimum it held firm to the positions of the *Syllabus*,[23] we would choose it without hesitation. But as things stand — given, that is, the mediocre and essentially bourgeois and parochial level to which practically everything that is confessional religion has descended, and given its surrender to modernism and the growing opening of the post-conciliar Church of '*aggiornamento*'[24] to the Left — for our men the mere reference to spirit can suffice, precisely as evidence of a transcendent reality. We must invoke it to inoculate into our force another force, to feel in advance that our struggle is not only a political struggle, and to attract an invisible consecration upon a new world of men and leaders of men.

* * *

These are a few essential guidelines for the battle we have to fight, directed especially to young people, so that they may grasp the torch and the commitment from those who have not fallen, learning from the errors of the past and knowing well how to distinguish and revise everything that was effected by and is still effected today by contingent situations. It is essential not to sink to the level of our adversaries, not to be reduced to manipulating simplistic slogans, and not to insist excessively on the past, which, even if worthy of being remembered, does not have the contemporary and impersonal value of the force-idea.[25] It is likewise mandatory not to yield to suggestions of a false politicising realism, which is the weak point of every 'party'. And, yes, our forces

---

23   The *Syllabus Errorum*, or *Syllabus of Errors*, was issued by Pope Pius IX in 1864, and was primarily an attack on modernist and liberal social trends.—Ed.

24   Meaning 'bringing up to date', the term was used by those who felt that the Vatican needed to update its ideas in keeping with modern trends, and was a crucial term used during the Second Vatican Council in the 1960s.—Ed.

25   Evola borrowed this concept from Georges Sorel, who used the term 'force-idea' to describe ideas, akin to myths, which could be used to motivate the masses.—Ed.

must also act in the hand-to-hand political struggle in order to create room for us to manoeuvre in the present situation and to limit the assault, otherwise unopposed, of the forces of the Left. But beyond that it is important, indeed essential to form an elite that can define an idea with intellectual rigor and intellectual intransigence in rapt intensity. We must unite around this idea and affirm it, especially in the form of the new man, the man of the resistance, the man who stands upright among the ruins. If it is granted to go beyond this period of crisis and unsteady and illusory order, the future will look to this man alone. The destiny that the modern world has created for itself is now overwhelming it. Even if it is not fated to be contained, if we stand by these premises, our inner state will be maintained. Whatever happens, what can be done will be done, and we shall belong to that fatherland that no enemy will be able to occupy or destroy.

ARTICLES ON ITALIAN FASCISM AND THE RIGHT IN OTHER LANDS

1930—1942

Identity Card

(1930)

It seems as though no one is allowed to circulate through the streets and public squares of the republic of letters nowadays without a regular 'identity card'. It does no good to declare yourself a foreigner or an 'outsider'. Passports do not seem to be permitted. You must be 'naturalised' and explicitly reject your own political views to fit the current measures. This, at least, is the decree of the prefects of the republic, presided over at no charge by the journalists who head the cultural pages.

This one time, let us satisfy these gentlemen and get ourselves in order.

Our journal, *La Torre*, was not founded in order to produce articles in praise of Fascism and the honourable Mussolini. Neither Fascism nor the honourable Mussolini would know what to do with such praise. This journal was founded to defend *principles* which would remain absolutely the same for us whether we found ourselves in a Fascist regime, or else in a Communist, anarchist, or republican one.

If these principles were transported onto the playing field of politics (with which they have nothing to do in themselves), they would bring about an order of qualitative differentiation, and thus of hierarchy, and thus of *empire* in the widest sense. Heroism and the warrior's dignity could only be justified from a superior point of view in our conception. In the same way we must oppose all that is democratic and levelling ferment in the most precise way and on all levels.

To the extent that Fascism follows and defends these principles, so far we can consider ourselves Fascists. So far and no further.

This 'style' is not the one in vogue now among the masses. Today, people begin by calling themselves Fascists and proceed to declare themselves for or against this or that idea, to the extent that the Fascist political line accepts or denies it — even when 'Fascism' is reduced to a taboo or a kind of entry ticket, which, once it is paid for, allows everyone to express opinions that are personal and divergent. We, on the other hand, begin with calling ourselves imperialists, in the integral sense, and anti-modern, and we support a political party, a nation, or a position — or we oppose them — to the extent that they obey or do not obey the imperial or aristocratic ideal. Let us say it again. We do not engage in 'politics'. We do not engage in it and we do not want to. We are defending ideas and principles.

We are neither nationalists nor internationalists, because the problem of empire is superior to both these modern ideologies. We are in favour of the idea of 'heredity', 'missions', or commitments that are obligatory for an empire for a given privileged race. This old nationalist ideology, once Hebrew and then German and Prussian, on the one hand, and, on the other, Giobertian and Mazzinian,[26] is for us only the fruit of vanity and a superstitious 'philosophy of history'. Empire belongs to the nation that makes itself worthy of it and especially does not talk about it, but *wants* it.

Moreover, we can only say that, if we cast an eye on the panorama of the modern world, compared with other nations, Italy, together with

---

26 Vincenzo Gioberti (1801–1852) was an Italian philosopher who favoured the independence of Italy from Austria and its unification under the leadership of the Pope. Giuseppe Mazzini (1805–1872) was a philosopher and Italian nationalist who led a number of failed insurrections intended both to gain Italian independence from the Austrian Empire and to unify Italy, although he remained at odds with others who fought for these goals due to his desire that Italy should become a republic rather than a kingdom.—Ed.

Germany, seems to us to possess certain possibilities for comprehending values and principles that could provide a foundation for empire in greater measure. We do not know whether such possibilities will succeed in conquering — or even only in limiting — the destructive action that modern 'civilisation' exercises powerfully on both these countries. We certainly hope so, especially in the name of our spiritual tradition and then for the good of the particular land we happen to live in.

With this we seem to have said enough, at least for now and especially because we do not desire to indulge in programs and declarations. There is only one 'myth' which we openly oppose: the myth under which spirituality and culture are supposed to be seen as virtually dependent parts of politics. We affirm for our part that it is politics that ought to be conditioned by spirituality and culture, if we want to avoid reducing politics to something small, empirical, and contingent. Since the honourable Mussolini has conceded that the Fascist Party card does not bestow intelligence on those who do not have it, and because we are not dealing with intelligence here, but with something superior, we still believe that our theses even on this subject are not so 'heretical', even in this context. As for the rest, we only hope that the margin of 'consistency' in our attitude, which can be acknowledged by anyone whose horizon is not restricted to a hand's breadth in front of his nose, will have the chance to become ever larger. Whether or not that will happen, as we have said, certainly does not depend on us.

Two Faces of Nationalism

(MARCH 1931)

It is a simply a fact that the World War, far from exhausting the process of clarifying the nationalisms of Europe and beyond, has carried this process to its acute phase. There is therefore today good reason to consider carefully the significance of this fact.

What is the meaning of nationalism in the context of a philosophy of culture? We ask ourselves this question, to which we believe we can give the following answer: *the nationalistic direction admits two possibilities that are theoretically distinct and antithetical, although in practice they are often confused with one another. One involves degeneration and regression, while the other instead leads to superior values — the prelude to resurrection.*

Let us see how we can render such an idea comprehensible, which in its mere statement seems so rich in consequences.

It is impossible to understand a phenomenon like nationalism without placing it in the context of a general historical vision that rests on the solid foundation of criteria of value.

Today a vision of this kind has a positive result: the progressive fall of political power from one to another of the planes that marked the qualitative differentiation of human possibilities in ancient cultures. The process has proceeded from the threshold of 'historical' times all the way to our day, and has particularly focused on Western political history.[27]

It is well-known that the analogy between the political organism and the human has a tradition of remote antiquity. However, in every higher form of bodily organisation, there is a hierarchical connection with four distinct functions. On the lowest level there are the undifferentiated energies of pure vitality. They are dominated from above by the functions of trade and the general organic economy. These in turn find in the *will* what moves and directs the totality of the body in space. Finally, at the top, there is a power of intellect and liberty, which is the centre and light of the whole organism.

Traditions existed which served almost as spiritualised bodies, not as creatures of necessity or temporal contingency for the great body of the states. They express a will for a division and a hierarchy of rigorously corresponding classes and castes. Corresponding to vitality, economic organisation, will, and spirit, there were the four distinct classes of slaves (workers), merchants, warriors, and finally the bearers of a simultaneously regal and sacerdotal authority. Each caste is set up hierarchically above another: the masses under the control and rule of experts in trade and the utilisation of natural and economic resources; and the merchants under the authority of warrior aristocracies, who in turn are gathered around a leading figure of a complete and dominating type who gave testimony, as it were, of something more than human in man.

The ancient Orient (India) and the Far East knew a similar type of social organisation. There was a partial similarity to this in ancient Greece and ancient Rome which is found in the political teachings of

---

27 The idea of the regression of the castes was first enunciated in our *Pagan Imperialism* (Rome, 1928). We found it in greater detail in the ideas of the honorable V Vezzani, which, however, still has no written exposition. Finally, René Guénon has expounded it in systematic form in *Spiritual Authority and Temporal Power* (Paris, 1929 [English edition: Ghent, New York: Sophia Perennis, 2001—Ed.). [Evola developed the ideas in *Revolt Against the Modern World*, Part II, chapters 14 and 15.—Tr.]

Plato and Aristotle, and which came to life again in the Catholic and feudal Middle Ages.

It is important to emphasise that this kind of organisation corresponded to the type of a *qualitative* hierarchy, and was characterised by its clarity of higher forms of interests and individualities. In the ancient Orient the two higher castes were called 'reborn', and so were the expressions of a spiritual elite. In this vision, the Warrior and the Aristocrat had a significance which was more 'sacred' than 'political'. Every hierarchy based on economy, work, industry, and administration remained restricted to the two lower castes, which were the equivalent to what is the bodily and vital part in a human organism.

So the hierarchy of the four castes represented the progressive steps of an elevation of individuality even perceptually, precisely by means of adhesion to forms of activity that are superior to those appropriate to everyday living. Compared to the anonymous masses, intent only on 'living', the organisers of work and wealth — the second caste — already represented the outline of a type, a 'person'. But we can already feel more clearly the form of what is 'more than living' in the heroism of the Warrior and the ethos of the Aristocrat — the third caste — and that of a being that gives himself a law that surpasses the natural element, which is instinctive, collective, and utilitarian. Finally, if the Ascetic, King, and Priest were mixed in a unique essence in the primordial notion of leadership, this unity designates a universal and almost supernatural fulfilment of personality; the complete expression of what does not have the force to liberate itself from the contingent in order to realise itself in the common man. To the degree to which such dominating figures, complete individuals, served as an axis for the entire social organism, this organism was like a body directed by the spirit, the temporal power and spiritual authority coincided, and the hierarchy was *legitimate*, in the absolute sense of the term.

The ideal model of this pattern, the basis of value, is independent of the degree and the form in which any particular society of the past could have realised it. Once the pattern is fixed, the realisation of the process of the progressive 'fall' from power in historical times becomes crudely evident. The era of the 'Sacred King' — of the natures that are simultaneously imperial and sacerdotal — already stands on the threshold of 'mythic' times. The peak disappears, power passes to the step immediately below — to the Warrior caste: monarchs of the lay type, military leaders, or lords of temporal justice.

Second collapse: the sunset of the great European monarchies, the decay of the aristocracies. Through revolutions (in England and France) and constitutions, they become empty remnants in respect of the 'nation's will.' Along with the parliamentary, republican, and bourgeois democracies, the rise of the capitalist oligarchies express the inevitable passage of political power from the second caste to the modern equivalent of the third caste — the merchants' caste.

Finally, the crisis of bourgeois society, the proletarian revolt, and the despotism of the masses that is established as purely collective, economic, and international entities forecast the final collapse, through which power passes to the last caste — the caste of those without names or faces, with the resulting reduction of every standard of living to the level of matter and number.

Another view: just like people who can no longer support the tension of the spirit, and then not even the tension of the will, of the force that moves the body — and they let themselves go — and then rise magnetically, almost like a soulless body, under the impulse of *another* force, which is barely seen, out of the shadows of pure vitality.

It is time to acknowledge the illusory character of all the myths of 'progress' and to open our eyes to reality. It is time to recognise the harsh destiny of spiritual destruction that has weighed on the West and that today is ripening its last fruits.

To reach our specific problem we need to emphasise that, in the centre of the involuted progress we have just described, the individual moves toward the collective, in strict dependence on the reduction of the interests from which the higher castes drew their legitimate hierarchical authority in favour of the interests of the lower castes, as we mentioned.

In reality a man can be free in himself only by adhering to his freedom of action. In the two symbols of pure Action (heroism) and pure Knowledge (contemplation, *ascesis*) that are supported by an aristocratic regime, the two higher castes open ways for man to participate in this 'super-worldly' order, which is the only one in which he can belong to himself and gather the integral and universal sense of personality. By destroying all interest in that order and by concentrating on practical and utilitarian goals, economic results, and all the other pursuits of the two lower castes, man disintegrates, loses his centre, and opens himself up to stronger forces that tear him out of himself and hand him over to the irrational and pre-personal energies of the collective life. It is rising above these which establishes the power of every truly superior culture.

This explains why the collective has been acquiring more and more power in the social forms of the recent past, so much as it were to return life to the totemism of primitive communities. Nation, race, society, and humanity rise today to the level of a mystic personality, and demand unconditional surrender and subordination from the individuals which form part of them, while at the same time hatred is fomented for those superior and dominating individualities in the name of 'liberty', who were the only ones in which the principle of subordination and obedience of individuals was sacred and justified. This tyranny of the group is not limited to affirming itself in what has a political and social character in the life of the individual. It arrogates for itself a moral and spiritual right. By insisting that culture and spirit are no longer disinterested forms of activity and ways to elevate the individual, but instead have become organs dependent on the collective temporal entity, it proclaims the morality of those who assert that the mind has sense and value only as an instrument in service to the body. Man, before identifying as personality or as ego, should identify with the social group, faction, or nation — this is one of the specific commandments of recent subversive ideologies, through which they cause the return of the relationship through which the primitive identifies with the *totem* of his own tribe or clan.

In the reawakening of the Russian race, in its assuming a universal prophetic mission for itself in Sovietism, we have a confirmation of the significance of this regression into primitive social levels, which is present in so many modern forms. This is precisely the opinion of those who see the definitive revolt of an Asiatic barbarian race in the new Russia, which rejects the bid for European civilisation undertaken for two centuries by the Tsars, and which is attempting to ally itself with the forms of social decomposition of the European world. Bolshevism is the revival of the ancient spirit of the Slavic race in modern form: a race without tradition that in its social mysticism, its amalgam of sensuality and spirituality, in the predominance of pathos over ethos, of instinct over rationality, leads us back to the forms of pre-personal lack of discrimination and Communist promiscuity found among primitive peoples.

The huge shock caused by the Great War has returned this element to a state of freedom and has made of it a terrible ferment of decomposition for the parts of Europe that are still healthy. In announcing the advent of the 'proletarian age', 'Soviet culture' has explicitly vowed itself to the destruction of the 'leprosy' of personality and liberty, 'the poisons of bourgeois society', and the principles of all evil; to the abolition not only of private property but of every independent thought and every 'movement that is supernatural and foreign to class interests'

(Lenin); to the advent of the 'omnipotent mass man', which alone ought to live and shape every manner of life and thought in individuals. The modern side of Bolshevism consists only in 'method'. Mechanisation and rationalisation are its preferred means to realise the 'mass man', which was already living mystically in the Slavic soul, in a purely economic, universal social regime. Soviet culture confronts — and is aware of it — another race, which equally claims a universal regenerative mission and the presumption to represent the final world of culture: America.

In America, instead of expressing the vitality of a people who remains in the pre-civilised state, the process follows the inflexible determinism that wants man, in the act of shutting himself off from every form of pure spiritualty in order to give himself over to the will of temporal things, to cease *ipso facto* to belong to himself, and becomes a dependent part of an irrational collective entity that he can no longer dominate. This is the state America has reached, following the ways of the sanctification of the temporal and the secularising of the sacred opened by the Protestant heresy. Carrying to its limit the ideals of the material conquest of the world that Europe had proposed, America blossomed — almost without noticing it — in making practical and physical every sense of power, sanity, activity, and personality, so as to construct a yet more fearful form of barbarism. Here the ascetic is considered as a waste of time, as an anachronistic parasite 'useless to society', while the Warrior is viewed as a dangerous fanatic who opportune humanitarian and pacifistic preventive measures ought to perhaps replace with a prize fighter. The perfect type, the spiritual champion, is instead the 'man who works, who produces', and every form of activity, even spiritual activity, is valued only in terms of 'work' and of 'productive work'. This is the most characteristic trait to show how it is precisely the representative type of the last of the ancient classes which stands at the top of such a society: the slaves destined to hard work. Here too, having renounced his spiritual personality, man ceases to have any value except for conditions imposed by the collective organisation, infected by the fever of producing, 'realising', and moving: conditions that, in addition, assume a moral and even religious value and tend to standardise the same souls in a collective and levelling *forma mentis*,[28] so as to scorn even the capacity to notice what level of degeneration all this constitutes.

These are the forms through which the cycle closes and the collapse is consummated. Russia and America are the two indicators and two converging faces of the same thing. The body moves backwards from the human organism, as it was when it was supported by the light and authority of the higher castes, to the type of a headless, subhuman organism: advent of the beast without a face.

We now possess all the elements we need to seriously confront the problem: *what is the meaning of nationalism in the modern world?*

One type of nationalism is clearly recognisable on the basis of what we have said. It is the level immediately preceding the international forms of economic and proletarian collectivism.

What is important in this nationalism is not the fact of the rise of a distinct national consciousness *vis à vis* others, but the fact that the 'nation' becomes a person, a being in itself, and the inability to surpass this right of blood and soil that concerns only the natural and sub-intellectual aspect of man, the impossibility of the individual to value himself otherwise than in terms of a given collectivity and a given tradition — these traits are elevated to ethical values. The fact of belonging to a 'nation' here confers a mystical halo on everything, which guards its inviolability and imposes respect for it. This sub-intellectual ethnic element not only refuses to acknowledge authority in superior principles, it reduces such principles to its own service. The 'nation'

---

28   Latin: 'way of thinking'.—Ed.

demands its own tribute — only later and subordinately is there room for reality, truth, and spirit. In certain nationalist forms, however, matters go beyond this. Every disinterested and objective criterion is accused of abstraction. The claim is made that even for reality, truth, and culture, it is impossible to ignore national tradition and political interest. This is why we hear talk of *our* scientific, philosophical, and even religious tradition.[29] Against everything that is not 'ours' and does not 'support the nation' there is placed a prejudice of lack of support or, at least, suspicious disinterest.

And just as there is no tolerance for the free manifestation of higher activities that might create a reality superior to what is ethnically conditioned, so in the ambiance of such a nationalism there is no respect for the superior personality except insofar as it is 'representative' of the nation. Born near the revolutions that have overthrown the remnants of the aristocratic and feudal regime, this nationalism therefore expresses a pure 'mob spirit'. It is a variety of the democratic intolerance for every leader that is not a mere tool of the 'popular will', dependent on its sanction in everything and for everything. It is easy to see that, between nationalism and a Soviet-style or American anonymity, there is basically only a difference of degree. In the Soviet version the individual is dissolved back into the original ethnic and national stocks; in the American one, the very differentiation that belongs to these ethnic stocks are overcome and a vaster collectivising and disintegration into the mass is produced. To take the people from one level to the other, it is enough that the mystique of race gives way to a structure of a purely economic and mechanical type. In such a structure, the last remnant of qualitative difference is eliminated through its impersonal

---

29 When we speak of tradition in a negative sense, as we are now doing, we mean to refer to that conception that does not imply any element that is truly intellectual, and therefore super-ethnic, and that — to use Chesterton's term, 'democracy of the dead' — represents an extension in time of what is the right presently accorded to majorities in respect to space: the right of the dead over the living, based on the fact of being dead members of the same race.

nature. With the rationalisation and mechanisation of social life, the ways remain virtually open for the advent of the mass man without a country. Given that the level of contemporary culture is precisely that of economic and mechanical power, and every criterion of value and greatness is reduced more or less directly to this level, it is perhaps only a question of time before this change comes to pass.

We can ask the following question, however: can nationalism assume another meaning? To this query we think we can respond affirmatively. We have said that nationalism appears as a form of passage to the sides of political dominion that lay in the hands of the third caste, but before the dominion of the lowest caste. This nature renders it susceptible to a double meaning. If we can meet this form of passage in the direction of a fall, we can also meet it in the direction of a recovery and of an eventual reintegration. Supposing that we have touched bottom, anyone who has found the strength to rise again would again meet up with nationalism — but this time another nationalism! As with the magnitude of 'vectors' in physics, this phenomenon can only be defined in terms of the factor of direction.

In the case of the first nationalism, the direction is towards collectivisation realised at the level of 'nation' — while in the second case it heads from collectivisation toward the reconstruction of a new *aristocratic* hierarchy.

To express the presuppositions of this second nationalism, it is especially important to pay attention to the words of Paul de Lagarde,[30] the noted exponent of German nationalism. The 'human' being is a step down from the 'national' being and the 'national' being is a step down from the being who is a 'person'. In other words, in respect to the quality 'humanity', the element of the difference 'nation' adds an

---

30   Paul de Lagarde (1827–1891) was a biblical scholar and orientalist at the University of Göttingen who was one of the first Pan-German theorists. Fervently anti-Christian and anti-Semitic, he called for the development of a new German national religion more reflective of Prussian values, and aggressive German expansionism.—Ed.

increment of value X, and the element of the single personality adds to this X a further increment of value Y. It is therefore the idea of a hierarchy that goes from the abstract to the concrete. The abstract is the collective, the general. The concrete, on the other hand, is the different, the individual. Compared to the amorphous mass of 'humanity', the rise of the differentiated national consciousness can therefore constitute a first step, but the national consciousness, the ethnic stock, ought to represent in its turn an unformed matter compared to individuals. When they are fulfilled and become themselves, and when they actualise themselves in forms of life superior to those conditioned simply by either blood or collective exigencies, they move from the state of chaos to one of cosmos, and from potentiality to act. And then the relationships are turned on their heads. The nation is no longer the end of the individual, but instead the individual as aristocratic or spiritual personality is the end of the nation insofar as the nation remains, as it were, its mother, almost in the same material condition that earth can represent in respect to a tree, which frees itself from the Earth with its higher parts and rises toward the free heights.[31]

This is the fundamental point of difference. To clarify it definitively, it is enough to return to the qualitative sense of the ancient hierarchy of the castes. Nationalism can never be a prelude to resurrection — not creating, but overcoming the mechanistic and collectivist state — unless we posit the bare necessity of restoring an order of values that cannot be reduced to what is practical, 'social', and economic, in order to confer on these higher values a primacy and direct authority over all the rest. Without this, no hierarchy exists, and without hierarchy,

---

31   Paul de Lagarde, *Deutsche Schriften* I (Dieterich: Göttingen, 1878), p. 164. ['Catholicism and liberalism never realised that an individual nation stands higher than humanity, and every individual member of a nation is more — that is, should be more — than just national, more than only what every fellow national as such is: that with nationalism, a very valuable X is added to humanity, and with the individual personality a much more valuable Y is added to this very valuable X; that humanity, nationality, ethnicity, family, and individuality are a pyramid whose peak reaches nearer heaven than its base', from Paul de Lagarde, *Deutsche Schriften* I (L. Horstmann: Göttingen, 1903), p. 141.—Tr.]

the return to a higher, spiritualised type of state is impossible. In fact, hierarchy does not simply mean subordination; it means the subordination of what has an inferior nature to what has a superior one. The inferior is everything that can be measured in practical, self-centred, and worldly terms. The superior is what expresses a pure and disinterested form of activity. Every other criterion is illusory and perverting. The case is 'illusory' whenever we think of hierarchy in the context of the economy alone and therefore on the basis of differences of money, political rank, of being a white collar worker, of class in the Marxist sense, and so on. The principle of a true hierarchy can arise only with the appearance of interests which are superior to the economic level as a whole. We must begin from the idea that we do not live to develop an economy, but that the economy is a means to an end. This end, however, is internal elevation, the deploying of the personality in an integral and 'otherworldly' sense. Hierarchy is therefore an absolute 'perversion' when it expresses subservience of what is not earthly to what is earthly, and when the spirit is made the tool of the body. Unfortunately with 'pragmatism' reigning on every level, even in science, with a vulgar Machiavellianism and general social climbing, we see this triumph of the earthly over the spiritual today in the great majority of cases. There is nothing more anti-hierarchical and even more anarchic than these bogus types of hierarchies.

In the context of a restorative nationalism we are dealing with the following: first of all, giving a formal order to everything that corresponds to the bodily, vital, or animal part of a human organism in the social whole, and that represents dominion over the two inferior classes: work, economy, and political organisation in the strict sense, creating an 'economic peace' that will bring about 'unwinding' and allow energies of a higher type to liberate themselves and act on a higher plane. Then men can begin reconstructing the second caste, which is that of the warrior aristocracy, with the monarch as the first of aristocrats.

It is a pure aristocracy in which the ideal of the higher formation of the personality can be realised. We should not look at the corrupt and degenerate stocks, against which an easy demagogic critique can be practiced. We should look at the original type of the Lord, as a being in which self-mastery, refinement, a disinterested attitude, culture, honour, loyalty, and especially the qualities of leaders have become a conquest consolidated on the sound basis of blood. Aristocracy is the necessary extension of positive nationalism, because if nationalism delineates the boundaries of blood and of an ethnic stock, aristocracy effects a selection and a further differentiation within such limits, leading from the general and collective towards the individual on a higher plane, which is the meaning of every real progress.

Once an aristocratic tradition has been reconstructed, the first glimmer of spirit will be infused into the body of the state, and nationalism, having achieved its proper task, can yield to higher forms which correspond to types of states that were maintained by the second caste. This will be characterised by an absolute personalisation of all relationships, of the passage from the mechanical to the organic, and from constriction to liberty. For instance, in other times, soldiers did not exist. There were warriors. They did not fight for the 'nation' or for 'right', but for their king. They did not obey 'social laws'; they were loyal to their own Lord. Anyone who submitted knew to whom he was submitting, and did it almost with pride. Responsibility was assumed by leaders and monarchs, instead of passing the buck to faceless entities or ideological taboos. Authority rested on the greatness of the personality and the capacity to devote oneself to what did not allow itself to buy or sell or measure in terms of what was 'useful'. It was no longer a question of 'living', but now of what was 'more than living'.

In turn, this will be the basis for a type of state of a higher form, but it is too distant for us to do more than sketch it in outline. Still, we can emphasise that just as a group of men can remain free and distinct as bodies, but can be united in a unique idea, so when the elites of the various stocks will be able to establish themselves on a level of true spiritual superiority, the paths will be virtually opened to a new universal culture. This does not mean 'internationalism', and much less a levelling humanitarianism — both of them creations of a materialistic mentality, since the reality and the political distinctions of the states stands at the same level as that of bodies, and we are not dealing here with the unity of bodies, but instead with the unity of culture and of really super-individual collectives. We find examples of this universality in the Catholic Middle Ages, the Roman Empire, and India, which demonstrate the possibility of a profound unity of culture and spirit along with the plurality of states or races that are ethnically distinct, and often even competing against one another. If we want to speak of a future *European* consciousness, we should speak of it only in these terms.

This, however, goes far beyond our present task, which is delineating the two opposing meanings of nationalism. We think we have made these two meanings quite clear. As for examining to what degree the variety of nationalisms present today and competing in the various states fall under one or the other meaning, this is a problem of an empirical character, which falls completely outside our consideration.

Paneuropa and Fascism: Colloquium with Count R N Coudenhove-Kalergi

(14 MAY 1933)

Count Coudenhove-Kalergi[32] is currently in Rome. He is the well-known promoter of the so-called 'Pan-European' movement and also the author of various distinguished works of philosophy and politics. Count Coudenhove came to Italy principally to meet Mussolini and to gain a first-hand impression of the part that the new Italy can have in respect to the problem of the unification of the lacerated political and spiritual reality of our continent. Since we had been in touch with him for some time, we found ways to have interesting meetings with the head of the Pan-European movement. He graciously agreed to the request of the honourable Farinacci to expound his most recent points of view concerning Europe directly in the pages of *Regime Fascista*.

'There are three great political problems, in relation to which Europe is today in crisis', Count Coudenhove tells us, 'that is, the problem of *constitutional reform*, the *social* problem, and the *European*

---

32 Count Richard Nikolaus von Coudenhove-Kalergi (1894–1972) was an Austrian whose mother was Japanese. A Mason, and a supporter of Woodrow Wilson's plans for Europe, he founded the Pan-European Union in 1922 with the intention of creating a united Europe based on conservative, aristocratic principles which would be capable of defending itself from Soviet incursions. He envisioned similar unions for the other regions of the globe, and believed that all races and social classes were destined to disappear as a result of the mixing that would take place within them. He remained active in his efforts toward uniting Europe for the remainder of his life.—Ed.

problem in the narrow sense. Among the various nations, Fascist Italy is the one which has given the greatest contribution to the solution of the first two points. Italy has already surpassed the problem of constitutional reform. It has given the necessary elements for the solution of the second problem, the social problem. It is destined to effectively confront the third and greatest problem, the European problem.'

We asked, 'Do you think that the Fascist solution to the constitutional and social problems can be valuable in solving the international one, as the Marxist and Bolshevik ones claim to be doing?'

'The Fascist constitution could have a value that is more than purely Italian, but could be more generally European', Coudenhove answers, 'insofar as it expresses a wise mixture of the authoritarian and aristocratic principle with what can be healthy in the democratic principle. It concedes room to justice and the enlightened command of superior personalities, and at the same time gives a solid base to the principle of identity, free adherence, and cooperation, by disciplining every power in the name of the higher idea of the nation. The European soul, as I conceive it, is characterised by three fundamental components: heroism, personality, and sociality. Since the Fascist solution includes all three in a wise equilibrium, so it presents itself as the most suitable one for assuming a character of European universality.'

Count Coudenhove continues, 'From the social point of view, the Fascist contribution consists essentially in the new corporative idea as an integrative surpassing of whatever could be positive in the famous Marxist myth of class struggle. In this regard, on the basis of a corporative reform realised within the principal states, I do not think we can exclude the idea of a future European corporative assembly, intended to study the most vital technical problems that are posed to the complex economy of our continent from a totalitarian viewpoint, and without restraint. This would have as its goal the attaining of the same results for which, on the contrary, people are now invoking the utopias of the Red international. On this same subject, it seems to me important to emphasise that, among the mistakes of the democratic regime, is allowing the parliamentary system to bypass politics. For me, separating the economic element from the political element is a necessity in a plan of renewal. This has already been achieved with the Fascist transformation of Parliament in the corporative chamber.[33] Naturally the goal here should not be a split, but the restoration of its own liberty to politics, rather than tying it down to the economy (as happens in Leftist ideology). This would instead permit politics to possess a wise, rationalising control from above on the economy when definite necessities present themselves.'

Returning to the idea of European solidarity, we ask the Count on what level he believes that such collaboration would be necessary.

'In respect of three principal unities: *economic, foreign affairs* — in the sense of a unified politics of the European nations in the face of non-European ones — and finally *military* unity. For a true European renewal, we absolutely need an agreement on these three points among the principal European powers. For the rest, there should remain the most ample independence of initiative.'

We know that Coudenhove has often been accused of pacifism. So we confront the question head on, by asking him what he meant by pacifism. Does he defend the generic and anti-virile ideal of peace, denying the higher, spiritual meaning that the experience and tests of a war can offer both to individuals and to the race? Or does he defend an inter-European pacifism, aimed only at unifying the various European forces, but not ruling out that a unified and concordant bloc of European power achieved in this way could find a renewed validity in an imperial and supremacist ideal of our races in confronting the remaining forces of the world? Coudenhove had no difficulty in

---

33   The Fascists had established a National Council of Corporations, which represented the interests of the industrialists and the workers but which remained under the control of the National Fascist Party, as well as the Grand Council of Fascism, which controlled the state's various institutions.—Ed.

acknowledging that his ideas move basically, and especially, in this second direction. He reminds us how often he has invoked internal European peace only because it is childish to persist in reciprocally paralysing the economic and military forces of the various European states, because a European defensive unity is necessary and salutary in the face of the three greatest anti-European powers: Russia, Asia, and America — and perhaps even an offensive one, as well.

'As for what concerns the more immediate and political side of the problem of European solidarity', Count Coudenhove added, 'we are dealing especially with counterbalancing the various forces, rather than trying to construct unilateral blocs of alliance. From this point of view I hold it essential for the pan-European idea to lay the basis for a Franco-Italian accord, and this for a double end: first of all, because only in this way can we reach an equilibrium between the two greatest elements of European culture, the *Latin* and the *German*, an equilibrium that would prevent the rise of hegemonic tendencies from either part. Second, before a Franco-Italian accord, the reasons for the Little Entente[34] would automatically collapse, and there would be an easy resolution of the problem of the small states of Eastern Europe. This last point is, in my opinion, rather important, because I believe that it is precisely from such states that the most likely incentive for a new conflagration could arise, which will certainly compromise the destinies of our entire culture.'

Naturally, Count Coudenhove is aware that our personal ideas would rather be oriented towards a European unification on the preliminary basis of an Italo-German bloc, adhering very strictly to ideals

---

34 In 1920, following the Versailles Treaty which ended the First World War, the Little Entente was a series of agreements for collective defence signed by Czechoslovakia, Rumania, and Yugoslavia in the event of an attack by Hungary, as it was feared at the time that Hungary might attempt to reabsorb these territories as part of a restoration of the Habsburg monarchy. Although this danger quickly passed, the Little Entente was maintained as a collective security arrangement against the Soviet Union and other threats, and later even began to serve as a means for economic integration. It gradually weakened and eventually collapsed in 1938.—Ed.

of an imperial and fascist type. Without disguising the obstacle to such perspectives that would be presented by the return of Germany to an exclusivist and essentially materialist racism, we ask the Count his view on the Franco-German question.

'This question effectively represents the fundamental obstacle to the realisation of a pan-European idea', Coudenhove answers, 'and I believe that the best way to resolve it is to arrive there indirectly. I mean, by means of that international politics of equilibrium and compensation of the European powers, about which I spoke a while ago. This has an especially tactical and preventative significance in respect to a possible Franco-German divergence, while maintaining the stability of the greater affinity that can exist between Germany and Italy in terms of political constitution and ethical formation. Here we see clearly the absolutely leading role reserved for your nation in respect to a possible "Pan-Europa". Because of its independence from the contingencies and crises of parliamentary regimes, Italy is today the nation that is most suited to conduct a far-sighted international politics. In practical terms, Italy has the possibility to become the umpire of relations between France and Germany, and this could become the first step on a new path. The moment has arrived for Fascism to direct its attention beyond the social and constitutional problem, concerning which its restorative cycle is already complete, to the problem of Europe, since, given the present situation and the recent upheavals of Europe's international politics, Italy is now really in a position to hold the keys to the destiny of our continent in its hands. This feeling for the right moment, joined to a Latin sense of equilibrium, is one of the most outstanding gifts of Mussolini's genius.'

'It is my firm conviction concerning Fascism's super-national mission that has brought me to Rome, where I have had the honour to be received twice and with all cordiality by the Duce', the Count finished. 'And I sincerely hope that the new Italy will remain faithful to its great tradition, working with every means at its disposal for this European idea, which had already been formulated by Dante, actualised spiritually by the Church of Rome, realised militarily by the Italian Napoleon, and finally renewed in a more modern way by the Mazzinian myth of the "New Europe".

Race and Culture

(JANUARY 1934)

Everyone knows the new importance that the *theory of race* has assumed today, especially because of the recent upheavals in German political ideology. Various discussions have emerged around this theory and its applications. For some, racism is the symbol of a new spiritualism. For others, it is the danger of a contaminating eruption of the biological element into the level of higher values. For some, it is a superstitious myth, since the idea of race is today something extremely undefined. For others, it instead represents an appeal to a new realism, the acknowledgement of the deepest substratum to which every organically creative action ought to appeal. With all this disagreement, some relevant considerations in the spirit of offering a clarifying explanation may be of interest, since it is not rare to observe connections, even unconscious ones, between the theory of race and the notion of the nation as *stock*, which is often taken up by many reactions against the dangers of recent cosmopolitan culture.

The premise of racism is decidedly pluralistic. 'Humanity' does not exist. *Many* races exist, and each of them has special gifts and characteristics, which cannot be changed without sinking into degeneration and decadence. According to deep biological and morphological laws, by which every single race is constrained, there corresponds its own soul, its own truth, and its own worldview, which can be now obvious, now latent, but does not change in essence in the course of centuries. From this arises a cultural and spiritual pluralism. For as many races as exist, there are just as many 'truths' and conceptions of the world. It is debated whether it is possible to speak in absolute terms of the justice, or lack of it, of a given worldview. It can be spoken of only in relation to a definite race, to its goals and its will to existence and power, because they are biologically innate and are sufficient for manifesting its life, while for a different race they could represent not only a serious danger, but their complete destruction. Racism therefore means acknowledgement of a definite differentiation of men as a basic fact: the relationship of a given group of men to a 'type'; purification of the stock that corresponds to it from extraneous ethnic and cultural elements; intimate adherence of the individual to the tradition of his own blood and to the 'truths' that are intimately linked to this blood; and elimination of all mixing.

This is the most recent form of the doctrine of race, in which two elements are acknowledged. Race is not considered only as a biological concept, but as a cultural concept. What, however, is the relationship between the two concepts? What is the ultimate reference point? In order to understand racism, to define the extent of its claims, and to integrate its positive aspects, we must confront this problem.

When racism is a reaction against an abstract universalism, against the Enlightenment and rationalist ideal of 'immortal principles valid for everyone', when it is the demand of a differentiated and organic type of truth, which is fitted to correspond to the deepest forces of our being — under this aspect, racism certainly represents something positive and healthy. But it must be acknowledged with equal clarity that racism becomes an aberration whenever it is felt that a defence and culture of race of an almost zootechnical type in its simply biological and empirical aspect is the equivalent *eo ipso*[35] of something creative

---

35   Latin: 'thereby'.—Ed.

and decisive. If the preservation and reintegration of the purity of race in an animal can be everything, in a man this can constitute a necessary condition under certain aspects, but in no case is it a sufficient condition, because man, as such, is not defined by the simple factor of 'race'.

This ingenuous materialism goes too far when there is talk simply of 'race', but even more so of a 'spirit' of race, passing therefore to a sort of *mystique of blood*. In reality, a mystique of race is what marks the lowest types of human society. It is the characteristic of the primitive, totemic type of society. The *totem* is the mystic spirit of the tribe and the order, elevated to a taboo and conceived as the intimate life-force of the individual members, as the soul of their souls and as the primary element within them. Here, the state in which the individual feels himself as a group, race, or tribe rules unconditionally and draws its fundamental distinctive traits from this feeling, not only biological ones, but psychic ones to an even greater extent. There is a type of racism that, as mystique of the blood *mutatis mutandis*,[36] leads back precisely to this level and therefore, despite all appearances, to forms of naturalistic and, in the last analysis, pre-personal life, and therefore constitutes a danger as serious as the universalism which it is combatting. Race in this case remains *nature*, and the claim it makes before the values of personality and culture must be deceptive and false.

In Germany, racists are always talking about *Aryanism*. Unfortunately, they are very far from an understanding of this concept that could lead them to a higher view. In fact, according to its original conception, *arya* is synonymous with *dvija*, that is, 'reborn' or 'twice born'. Its nature is defined by a definite act: initiation. The *Manava Dharma Shastra*[37] (11.172) actually declares that, when the *arya* neglects

---

36 Latin: 'the necessary changes having been made'.—Ed.

37 The *Manava Dharma Shastra*, or *Laws of Manu*, is one of the oldest and most important Vedic texts, describing how law and social structures should be maintained.—Ed.

this act, he has no way to actually distinguish himself from the *shudra*, that is, the element that constitutes the dark and servile castes, which were originally formed from aborigines conquered by the Aryans.[38] If we understand 'initiation' not in its absolute traditional sense, which is related to interior horizons that are today almost completely forgotten, but in its analogical sense of *culture* — that is, of an action by which the individual frees himself from his own base nature, reacts against it, and imposes a higher law upon it — then we have the fundamental premise for reaching a more elevated conception of the doctrine of race.

When a being owes everything that gives form and support to his life to the forces of instinct and blood, he still belongs to 'nature'. In the case of a human being, he can still develop superior qualities on this basis, but such qualities will always remain an expression of nature, not a possession of his personality, like the splendid racial traits that can be found in a tiger or every 'thoroughbred'. The passage from the kingdom of *nature* to that of *culture* (in the aforesaid classic sense, and not the modern sense of instruction, erudition, etc.) takes place only when a different power is manifested that stands in relation to the simple element of race as the soul stands in relation to the body formed in its image. In this way, the laws and instincts of organic nature are no longer the basis and principle of the spiritual faculties and 'truths' that belong to a given blood, but *vice versa*. Here we find a *style* that assumes 'nature' as the primary matter and vehicle, but does not allow itself to be reduced to nature, and vouches for the presence and formative action of an element of meta-biological order. *Exactly this*

---

38 According to some versions of the Aryan Invasion Theory (AIT), which was generally accepted at the time Evola was writing, Indian civilisation arose when lighter-skinned Aryans from the north invaded India, which was then the home of darker-skinned Dravidians known as the Indus Valley civilisation, and conquered it, and the Vedic caste system was established, in part, in order to differentiate the Dravidians from the Aryans and maintain the purity of the former. Today the AIT is in dispute, and many scholars question if it actually transpired in this manner, or indeed whether it happened at all, the archaeological record being inconclusive. —Ed.

*'style' constitutes what can be called race in a higher sense, with reference
to man as man and not as animal, 'superior' or not.*

In the animal kingdom and primitive societies, race belongs to the
biological level, and begins and ends appearing as a mere fact, imper-
vious to any creative initiative and predetermined collectively. When
we talk of man, though, 'race' no long stands on this level, although it
manifests itself in it, rendering itself visible through a typical and well-
determined complex of qualities, attitudes, dispositions, sensibilities,
and interests, which, however, in the last analysis, are only signs and
symbols for the fact of spiritual nature: *culture as the deep substratum
of race.*

When the ancient traditions speak of the 'divine' origins of certain
races; when in our classical antiquity the patricians based their claim
to dignity on the basis of the fact of having a sacred heredity united
to dignity of blood, which had been awakened to life by a 'hero' or
semi-divine forefather and which was connected to a ritual tradition;
when *arya* counted as a synonym for 'reborn' or the Iranian-Aryan
dominating castes defined themselves through participation in particular forms of a 'heavenly fire', and so on — in all these echoes, once we
overlook the mythological and symbolic aspect, we rediscover exactly
these meanings. And so we reach the opposition between cultures in
which race signifies *culture,* and those in which race signifies *nature.* If
we should arrive at the problem of racial differences beyond the purely
empirical ones, and beyond the problem of the distinction between
superior and inferior races — it is precisely in these terms that it will
be necessary to speak. As a man is worthier of the name, man, insofar
as he knows how to give a form and law to his character, tendencies,
and actions — a form and law that end with reflecting even his exterior
figure — so a race stands so much higher insofar as its ethnic tradition
is accompanied by a dominating spiritual tradition, almost as body
and soul, and insofar as both are found in an unbreakable union.

On the other hand, today's revival of the inferior, naturalistic concept of race can only work in a negative way. In fact, there exist today values of 'civilisation', if not of spirituality, or at least of intellectuality, which, can only appear as extrinsic matters to be subordinated to the values of 'blood' and 'race' before this concept. At the centre, and as taboo, a purely cumulative and collectivistic entity is placed. A culture is also allowed, insofar as it is made an instrument of nature, with the consequent subordination of every value, every truth, and every dignity of personality to the race's coarsest will to existence and power. In this way a *radical irrationalism* takes the upper hand, as a deviation that is as dangerous for the elements of every true human greatness as for the anti-racist and internationalist rationalism it fights.

If it is natural that, in the context of the naturalistic conception of the hygiene of the race, the external defence of simple ethnic purity, together with a fundamental distrust of everything that is of the 'other' — this is presented as a universal panacea — for practical purposes, we remain here in the realm of pure myth. If the true centre is race as 'nature', given the present state of race-mixing, looking for racial elements fit to serve as solid reference points for racist hygiene in their purity is in fact a hopeless undertaking. At most, a *negative* action will be possible, meaning the prevention of further mixing, but not *positive* action, meaning the creative reintegration of the original power of blood in the whole of ethnic stocks that have been changed and are vacillating in an individualistic and 'civilised' world. It is no use getting in touch with ancient traditions and ancient mythologies of the stock on the basis of the 'mystique of blood'. Unless the plans are changed, all this can only be effective today in terms of aiding the rise of the irrational and primitive, that is, of elements that are lower and not higher than the world of common culture. Even if it may be harmful in its deviations, however, it could also furnish support for the intimate formation of Western man.

We now pass to another conception, that is, to the idea of race not as nature, but as culture. In this understanding, the defence of race implies a double condition. Race here corresponds to the refinement, selection, even the formation, realised in nature, of a higher power, and transmitted through ethnic biological heredity. It is evident that we are dealing here with preserving and defending this same heredity, but additionally and especially it is necessary to keep this spiritual tension or internal, formative soul alive, since it is this which raised this material all the way to that definite form. This is the source of the error of racists like de Gobineau:[39] the decadence of a culture is not — as they claim — the result of the mixture of the race that originally called it to life with other races. The true cause is not ethnic, biological, or demographic degeneration. The truth is rather that a race with its own culture degenerates when its spirit declines, when the intimate tension to which it owed its 'form' and its 'type' disappears. It is then that the race changes or is corrupted because it is damaged in its root. Then the ethnic and biological elements are deprived of the close link that held them together in the unity of form, and the first alteration will suffice to produce rapid degeneration and corruption. The collapse and change of the stock is not only moral, but more than that, ethnic and biological. In this case it returns to the level of the simple forces of nature, and succumbs to its own contingency on this level.

Certainly, the preservation of ethnic purity ought to appear — where talk about it corresponds to reality — as the most favourable condition so that the 'spirit' of a race can maintain itself in its original force and purity, just as in the individual the health and integrity of the body are warrants for the full efficiency of the higher faculties. Otherwise, a man who is morally constituted and strong in his will does not have

---

39   Joseph Arthur Comte de Gobineau (1816–1882) was a French novelist who is also credited with writing the first theory of modern racialism, *The Inequality of Human Races*. In it, de Gobineau first asserted the idea of Aryan supremacy, although his ideas were greatly at odds with the later views of the National Socialists.—Ed.

a proper internal life because of his external weakness. Analogously, when a race has a truly strong and complete culture for its soul and basis, the simple fact of its contact with and even mixing with other races far from simply signifies its destruction. On the contrary, its sprit may work like an invisible and irresistible ferment on the foreign elements, so as to reduce them to the same type. There is no need to mention the historical examples of this process, which are known to everybody — *the process of the passage from the idea of race to the idea of empire.*

This is a very important element for the opposition we mentioned above. Where the naturalistic idea of race can only lead to a limiting particularism, to a petty and jealous exclusivism synonymous, in most cases, with fear before horizons whose extent seems beyond one's capacity — in the higher idea of race, the potential of the imperial function is inherent, which surpasses both levelling internationalism and a disintegrating racism. Mussolini correctly writes, 'For Fascism, the tendency to empire, that is to say the expansion of nations, is a manifestation of vitality, its contrary (the stay-at-home attitude) is a sign of decadence.'[40] The element that makes *a* race, truly and spiritually, inevitably leads it beyond itself.

There is a final consideration. It is an element inherent in the very concept that every 'return' to race as nature must have a character that is collectivist and, in its political assumptions, demagogic. This demagogy disguises itself in mystic vestments and authoritarian structures. It is a return of the tyrannical power of the pure *demos*,[41] the advent of the 'spirit of the mob', and the reincarnation of the 'primordial horde'.

The 'return' to race in the other conception means instead returning to its internal tradition, and is closely connected to the idea of a

---

40   'The Doctrine of Fascism', in Benito Mussolini, *Essays on Fascism* (London: Black House Publishing, n.d.), p. 44.—Ed.

41   Ancient Greek: 'the people'.—Ed.

leader [*Duce*] and a *hierarchical order*. If the race is a formation from above, a triumph of 'culture' over 'nature', the renewal of the primordial formative power that is sleeping in its breast can, practically speaking, only be effective in an *élite* with a clear gaze, a firm will, and an unshaken superiority; an *élite* that will act in two directions. First of all it will act in a function of order, authority, formation, and articulation of all that is social in terms of a state that becomes the entelechy, that it, precisely the vital formative principle of the internal and of the nation. In second place, it will act with an *action of presence*. We mean that its heads, as outstanding incarnations of the 'type' of the race, present themselves as 'realised ideals', and as such rekindle a power lying deep within individuals. They are the source of the magic of enthusiasm and animation they arouse in terms of true recognition and heroic and conscious dedication, rather than a passive, collective suggestion. This was exactly the idea that Mussolini expressed in speaking of the stock not as quantity, collective, or naturalistic unity, but on the contrary as a 'multitude unified by an *idea*', an idea that 'is realised in the consciousness and will of the few or even of one only; an ideal which moves to its realisation in the consciousness and will of all'.[42] Then the multiple forces of a stock, which have become fatally directed towards change and disintegration when they were deprived of inner support and abandoned to the contingency of material factors, whether ethnic or political in the narrow sense, rediscover a solid and living point of unity in a form of galvanising contact.

This is the concluding point. To the return of the mystique of the 'primordial horde', to racist ideology that subordinates everything to the right of a mere community of blood, soil, and origin, there is opposed the *aristocratic* conception and tradition of race as a manifestation of a force of 'culture', a tradition that finds its natural crowning achievement in the Roman idea of *imperium*.

---

42   'The Doctrine of Fascism', p. 30.—Ed.

What does the Spanish Falange Want?

(JANUARY 1937)

While everyone has followed the phases of the Spanish Civil War with lively interest, the ideas that animate the insurrection of the Spanish national forces against Communism are less well known, because many believe that the positive ideological phase in revolutions always develops at a later period.

This is not our opinion. We believe that the best soldier is the one who fights with precise knowledge of his cause and, even if the ideas are apprehended or intuited confusedly rather than clearly formulated, ideas are the primary reality in every really important historical upheaval. We are therefore grateful to Alberto Luchini[43] for having informed us about the doctrinal program of one of the principal Spanish nationalist tendencies, the so-called Spanish Falange.[44] He makes their terms lively and dynamic with the resources of a style of translation that is really amazing, and I might say worthy of a magician in its

---

43   Dr Alberto Luchini was the head of the Race Bureau of the Ministry for Popular Culture, who collaborated with Evola on a magazine, *Sangue e Spirito*. Luchini also worked with Ezra Pound, assisting him in his translation of Confucius.—Ed.

44   The Falange was founded by José Antonio Primo de Rivera in 1933. In 1937, following the execution of Primo de Rivera during the Spanish Civil War, the leadership of the Falange passed to Francisco Franco, who unified the movement with other nationalist groups, stripping it of much of its fascist character.—Ed.

vigour, precision, and happy improvisation.[45] It deals with a general profession of political faith, whose formulation seems to be due to José Antonio Primo de Rivera[46] or the writer Giménez Caballero.[47] This program has almost flabbergasted us for its wealth of spiritual content, so much so that we believe it appropriate to bring it to the attention of the Italian public and relate its main points in synthesis.

First point. Neither linguistic unity, nor ethnic or territorial unity, are considered sufficient to give real content to the idea of the nation. 'A nation is a predestined, cosmic unity.' This is also affirmed as being true of Spain: a unity, a destiny, 'an entity subsisting beyond every person, class, or collectivity in which it is realised,' not only but moreover above 'the complex quantity that results from their aggregation'. We are dealing with the spiritual and transcendent idea of the nation, which is opposed to every form of collectivism — of the Right or the Left — and every mechanistic philosophy. 'As a true entity of its own perfect truth, a living and sovereign reality, Spain consequently tends toward its own definite goals.' In regard to this, there is not only talk of 'a return in full to worldwide spiritual collaboration', but even more of a 'universal mission of Spain', and of the creation, from the side of the 'solar unity' which it represents, 'of a new world'. Certainly, in regard to this last point, and good intentions apart, there remains a question mark.

What Spain could say, today or even tomorrow, in the place of a universal idea, is in fact very unclear. The reality, however, is that here there is the effect of a precise logic. It is not in fact possible to spiritually assume the idea of a nation without being instinctively led

---

45   *I Falangisti spagnoli* (Florence: Beltrami, 1936). (Portions of Primo de Rivera's writings were translated into English in *The Spanish Answer: Passages from the Spoken and Written Message of José Antonio Primo de Rivera* [Madrid: Editorial Almena, 1964], reprinted as *José Antonio Primo de Rivera: The Spanish Contribution to Political Thought* [London: Black Front Press, 2013]).—Ed.

46   José Antonio Primo de Rivera (1903–1936) founded the Falange in 1933. In 1936, he was arrested and executed by the Spanish republican government.—Ed.

47   Ernesto Giménez Caballero (1899–1988) was a Spanish writer and film director who became an early supporter of the Falange, and sat on its council. He made attempts to wed Primo de Rivera's sister to Hitler, believing that this would 'soften' the *Führer*.—Ed.

to surpass its particularism and conceive it as the principle of a super-national spiritual organisation, with the value therefore of universality, even when there may be very little at its disposal to give a concrete and effective form to such a demand. And vice versa: every particularist restriction of a national idea always leads to the emergence of a latent materialism or collectivism.

Let us pass to the more strictly political part of the program. Falangists say 'no' to the agnostic state, which is a passive spectator of the national public life or, at most, a police agent in the grand style. The state ought to be authoritarian, a state of everybody, total and totalitarian, justifying itself in this form, however, always with reference to the ideal and perpetual notion of Spain, independent of any class or party interest.

The extirpation of parties and their annex, the parliamentary gymnasium, follows naturally from this view. The Falangists, however, under the power of the centuries-old tradition of their fatherland, seem to also stand on guard against these excesses of totalitarianism that, in their work of levelling and uniformity, threaten to make of some nationalist tendencies nationalised facsimiles of Bolshevism. This is why Falangists insist on the necessity for organic human groups, alive and vital, to articulate the true state and to be its solid foundations. They therefore intend to defend the integrity of the family, the basic cell of social unity; communal unity, the basic cell of territorial unity; and, finally, the professional and corporative unities, the basic cells of a new national organisation of work and organs for surpassing the class struggle.

In regard to this last point, the adherence of Falangists to the fascist corporative idea is complete. 'The union and corporative categories, up until now unable to participate in the national public life, will have to rise into immediate organs of the state, once the artificial barriers of Parliament and the political parties are beaten down.' The collectivity of producers as an organic and unified totality will understand themselves as 'totally interested in and committed to the common, unique, and outstanding endeavour', an endeavour in which first place must always remain assuredly given to the general national interest.

It is perhaps no accident that the chapter that follows right after this one deals with the human personality and denounces the danger that a nation might transform itself completely into a kind of 'experimental laboratory', as follows from the logical consequences of Bolshevism and mechanistic philosophy. The emphasis given to the dignity of the human personality, to be clearly distinguished from individualistic judgment, seems to us one of the most salient and characteristic traits of the program of the Spanish Falange. Let us cite what is significant on this topic: 'The Spanish Falange discerns in the human personality, beyond the physical individual and physiological individuality, the spiritual monad, the soul ordered to perpetual life, the instrument of absolute values that is an absolute value in itself.' From this vision comes the justification of a fundamental respect for 'the dignity of the human spirit, for the integrity and liberty of the person, a profound liberty legitimated from above, which can never be translated into the liberty to conspire against civil society and undermine its bases'. This declaration decisively overcomes one of the major dangers of the anti-Marxist counterrevolution: the danger, that is, of harming the spiritual values of the personality at the moment of justly striking the liberal and individualist error in its political and social seat.

It is hardly necessary to emphasise that by accepting these premises, Falangists repudiate every materialist interpretation of history, since they conceive of spirit as the origin of every truly decisive force. Their Catholic profession of faith is equally natural. The Catholic interpretation of life is, historically speaking, the only one that is 'Spanish'. Every labour of national reconstruction must refer to it. This does not mean a Spain that must again submit to the interferences, intrigues, and hegemony of ecclesiastical power, but a new Spain, animated by that 'Catholic and universal sense' that has already led it 'against the alliance of ocean and barbarism to the conquest of unknown continents'; a Spain penetrated through and through with the religious forces of the spirit.

Falangists fight for these ideas as 'volunteer warriors' committed to 'conquer Spain for Spain'. These ideas, in their general line, seem to us perfectly 'in order'. They are clear and can have value as solid reference points. If they have really penetrated the Spanish national movement, we have two reasons to sincerely wish them a complete, rapid, and definitive victory: not only for the negative anti-Communist and anti-Bolshevik side, but even more for the positive which can follow in the totality of a new, hierarchical Europe, a Europe of nations and of personality.

The Spiritual Meaning of Autarchy

(1 March 1938)

In today's world it often happens that the force of circumstances and of those 'positive causes' which in many circles are valued so highly, seem to determine situations that appear to derive all their meaning from them, but that to a sharper eye are revealed to be susceptible to incarnating a higher value as well, and in so doing elevate themselves above the order of pure contingency.

We used the word 'susceptible' intentionally, since we wanted to indicate the character of 'possibility', and not of necessity, which belongs to this higher assumption. There are many cases in which destiny offers us something, without our noticing it and being able to take advantage of it. And in many other cases, in both individual and collective life, the force of things acts like a horse tamer, who, although he has real love for the horse, is compelled to whip it repeatedly, because the horse cannot understand him. The horse is diligently accomplishing all the elements of the exercise, but is always stopping at the last hurdle, which he could easily have jumped over with a small effort if he had understood. In an age in which the eye is hypnotically fastened to the material level, the level of 'positive reality', painful cases of this type occur with great frequency. People receive 'blows' from every direction, without succeeding in understanding and coming to the right orientation. The 'lessons of experience' serve to accumulate facts laboriously and organise them in different ways for our practical goals, but they do not serve to help us realise their *meaning*; they do not serve, that is, *to wake us up* and, once we are awake, to guide us to the right reaction.

The famous saying, 'the economy is our fate', is a sad sign of an epoch that, unfortunately, has not completely disappeared below the horizon. An obvious falsehood in every period of normal history and culture, this principle *became* true after man destroyed all the traditional values one after another, and all the higher reference points that used to preside over his decisions and actions. The ubiquity of the economy is the sign of an abdication, almost in the same way that the ubiquity of psychophysical automatism in hypnosis presupposes the suspension of the conscious faculties and, in general, of the personality.

Naturally, as a formula this principle is today obsolete, at least among the factions of the Right. 'Fascism', as Mussolini said, 'still believes in sanctity and heroism, that is to say in acts in which no economic motive, immediate or remote, operates'.[48] He refuses to admit that economic activities by themselves, to the exclusion of all other factors, suffice to explain all of history. Another well-known formula is that acknowledging the power of the economy must be joined to acknowledging that man is not its object, but its subject. All this is evident, intuitive, and natural. It is the opposing view that has all the characteristics of a real ideological anomaly.

So much for theory. In practice, unfortunately, things go rather differently, because 'the spirits you have evoked you will not easily dismiss', as Goethe noticed.[49] While on the one hand we cannot avoid rejecting the principles of the Idealist revival, on the other we often find ourselves compelled to deal with very precise practical necessities, and bearing them in mind is an equally sacred commitment for

---

48   'The Doctrine of Fascism', p. 36.—Ed.

49   '*Die ich rief, die Geister, Werd' ich nun nicht los.*' From 'Der Zauberlehrling'.—Ed.

anyone who does not want to cut his own nation off from reality and lead it on short notice to ruin. In such a dualism, the more tragic side is its degenerating into an absolutely real antinomy. Sometimes people are compelled to shut up for the moment, or to delay the idea in the name of the needs of economic, financial, and commercial forces that are demanded by the most essential interests of the nation. Idea and reality do not always run in parallel lines in contemporary politics. This is a matter of indifference where the idea is a pure simulacrum, a mere myth, subordinate to Mammon, but it is very serious where we are dealing with a real idea.

Anyone who examines the developments of recent years can come to believe that *autarchy* is more than a principle; it is the necessary consequence of a definite general political and economic situation. For many people, this presently constitutes an authentic scandal and the height of irrationality, since rationality for them has been recognised in the 'division of labour' and trade with a sufficient margin of liberty and equality of tariffs. It is absurd, they say, to establish a system on principle according to which some people are compelled to excogitate every resource and to tighten their belts to live 'autarchically', and other people are instead amazed by their own wealth. From this we see a 'creature of necessity' in autarchy, determined by the violent and irrational intervention of politics in the economy.

The ease with which a similar view can be overturned by undoubtedly materialist traits is indeed surprising. We can wonder, therefore, if the opposite system is 'rational' and 'sensible', the system of the so-called free market, which amounts to the brute fact in which a certain larger economic power, based primarily on the control of raw materials by some people, establishes the iron links of a supine dependence of other people on the first group, precisely through the 'necessity' and 'rationality' of the 'normal' economic process. From a higher point of view, this is the most repugnant of these illogicalities, and an uglier yoke than any tyranny directed at the individual.

People today who refuse to be caught in the gears of such machinery, and who have chosen autarchy for a principle, are people who have awakened to something spiritual, people who have shown that they possess sensibility for values that are not reducible to those of the stomach and those annexed to it: this is already the principle of a liberation. If they have been brought here by necessity (and by necessity we ought to include everything that refers to a realistic politics alone), we ought to acknowledge that necessity, in this case, has had exactly this providential function, to which we referred at the beginning, and that a single step suffices, with the right reaction, to raise oneself to an effectively spiritual consciousness.

Etymologically, autarchy means a person 'has his own first principle in himself'. The only free man — the ancients used to say — is one who has his own first principle in himself. The entire question turns on the meaning of this freedom. The current interpretations are well known: they are found in the financial field on the one hand and the military field on the other. Economic autarchy guarantees us a margin of liberty concerning the politics of currency; it allows us to regulate and defend our money. Secondly, economic autarchy is a necessary premise for modern war. Without economic independence, the conduct of a modern war is seriously prejudiced; it is reduced to something like a game of chance that either succeeds on the spot (that is, on short notice) or leads to ruin, since the technical and military machinery of a modern war cannot be nourished on its own, even without mentioning the possibility of a blockade.

These are two excellent reasons, but the third, which to our way of thinking is the most important one, is forgotten. Autarchy has the value of a principle, in the highest sense of the term, because it is the *conditio sine qua non*[50] for a liberty of alliances and hostilities on a basis that is not materialist (pragmatic) but ethical. In fact it is evident that the greater the degree to which a nation will succeed in establishing itself as economically autarchic, the greater will be its capacity to follow an idea, if not finally an ideal, in its complete foreign politics; in other words, the greater will be its capacity to choose friends and enemies independently of crude opportunity and brute necessity. Autarchic nations would be the only ones in a condition to form alliances justified by true principles, by ideal and spiritual affinities, instead of a pure and changeable juncture of interests. The one thing, certainly, does not exclude the other, and the ideal condition undoubtedly exists when it results from the conjunction of the two levels. The case of an imperfect conjunction is exemplified by the dark epoch of materialism and economism, from which we are only now escaping, and which was characterised by a cynical, cold, and ready subordination of the idea to self-interest. The new epoch, if it does not betray itself, and if it should really deserve to be called new, will be characterised by the opposite principle, that is, by an active decision of nations and by a decision from above, on the basis of these possibilities of independence and mobility, which proceed from the highest level of autarchy sensibly realisable in each of them.

The day it reaches this level, the positive side of autarchy will appear clearly. Even if this principle has at first been imposed mostly from outside, and demanded of us force and discipline, the new attitude will allow us to judge affairs from a very different point of view: coercion on the part of 'history' will be understood as the only means available to give a higher instinct that is not yet conscious of itself a first sense of the right direction.

---

50   Latin: the essential conditions for something.—Ed.

Legionary Asceticism: Colloquium with the Head of the Iron Guard

(22 MARCH 1938)

O ur car is speeding away from that curiosity that is downtown Bucharest: a collection of small skyscrapers and modern buildings, mostly of the 'functionalist' type, with exhibits and department stores halfway between Parisian and American in style. The only exotic element is the astrakhan caps which are frequently worn by the police and businessmen. We reach the northern station and drive down a dusty provincial road bordered by little buildings reminiscent of old Vienna. Heading along a straight line, the road reaches the country. After a full half-hour, the car unexpectedly swerves to the left, takes a country road, and then stops in front of a virtually isolated building surrounded by fields. It is the so-called 'Green House', the home of the Captain of the Rumanian 'Iron Guard'.

'We built it with our own hands', the legionnaires accompanying us say with a certain pride. Intellectuals and artisans worked together to build the residence of their leader, almost with the significance of a symbol and a rite. The style of architecture is Rumanian. On each side there is a long portico that almost gives the impression of a cloister.

We enter and walk up to the second floor. We are met by a tall, slim young man in a sports suit with an open face, which immediately gives an impression of nobility, power, and loyalty. This is Corneliu

Codreanu, Captain of the Iron Guard. His type is characteristically Aryan-Roman — he seems like a figure from the ancient Aryan, Italian world. While his grey-blue eyes express the hardness and cold will that belong to leaders, in the totality of his expression there is at the same time a singular note of idealism, self-possession, power, and human understanding. His way of conversing reflects these characteristics. Before answering questions, he seems to become self-absorbed and detached, then, suddenly, he starts talking, expressing himself with an almost geometrical precision in well-articulated and natural phrases.

'After a horde of journalists of every nation and colour who are only capable of asking me questions about the politics of the moment, your visit is the first time — I say this with satisfaction — that someone visits me who is interested, first of all, in the soul and the spiritual nucleus of our movement', Codreanu says. 'For the other journalists I have discovered a formula that satisfies them and means almost nothing: *constructive nationalism*.

'A man is composed of an organism, that is, an organised form, then of vital forces, and then of a soul. The same can be said about a people. The national construction of a state, although it naturally includes all three elements, for reasons of various qualifications and heredity, can be inspired especially by one of these particulars.

'In my opinion, in the fascist movement, the element of the state is predominant, and is the equivalent of the organised form. The source is the formative power of ancient Rome, mistress of justice and political organisation, of which the Italian is the purest heir. In National Socialism the emphasis is on what connects to the vital forces: race, the instinct of race, and the ethnic and national element. In the Rumanian legionary movement, the accent falls especially on what corresponds to the element of soul in an organism, or the spiritual and religious aspect.

'This is the source of the distinctive trait of the various national movements, although in the end they contain all three elements and neglect none of them. The specific character of our movement comes to us from a remote heredity. Already Herodotus called our progenitors, "the immortal Dacians". Our Getic and Thracian ancestors had a faith, already before Christianity, in the immortality and indestructability of the soul, which proves their orientation towards spirituality. The Roman colonisation added the Roman spirit of organisation and form to this element. All the successive centuries have made our people wretched and broken into pieces. However, just as even in a sick and ill-tempered horse one can recognise its thoroughbred nobility of race, so even in what it has become yesterday and today, the Rumanian people can recognise the latent elements of this double legacy.

'And it is this legacy that the legionary movement wants to awaken', Codreanu continues. 'It comes from the spirit. It wants to create a spiritually new man. When this task has been realized in the "movement", we await the awakening of the second legacy, that is, the politically formative Roman power. So spirit and religion are for us the starting point. "Constructive nationalism" is the destination and almost the consequence. Connecting the two points is the mission of the ascetic, and at the same time heroic, ethics of the "Iron Guard".'

We ask Codreanu about the relation of the spirituality of his movement to the Orthodox Christian religion. He answers:

'In general we aim to resurrect, in the form of a national consciousness and a lived experience, what has often been mummified and become the traditionalism of a somnolent clerisy in this religion. We find ourselves in a fortunate condition, because the dualism between faith and politics is foreign to our religion, which is articulated nationally and so can furnish us with ethical and religious elements without imposing itself as a merely political entity. The Iron Guard movement takes a fundamental idea from our religion: that of *ecumenicity*. This means the overcoming of every abstract and rationalistic internation-alism and universalism. The ecumenical idea is that of *societas* as a unity of life and a living organism, living together not only with our people but also with our dead and with God. Realising such an idea in the form of an effective experience is the centre of our movement. Politics, party, culture, and so on are only the consequences and deri-vations of this idea. We must bring this central reality back to life and so in this way reinvent Rumanian man, so that we can then proceed to likewise construct the nation and the state. An important point is that the presence of the dead in the ecumenical nation for us is not abstract, but real. We cannot separate ourselves from the presence of our dead and especially our heroes. As forces liberated from the human condi-tion, they penetrate and sustain our highest life. The legionnaires meet periodically in little groups, called "nests". These meetings follow spe-cial rites. Every meeting begins with the call to all our fallen comrades, and those present respond with "present!" For us this rite is not just a ceremony and allegory, but a real evocation.

'We distinguish individual, the nation, and transcendent spiritual-ity', Codreanu continues. 'In heroic dedication we consider what leads from one to the other of these elements, all the way to a higher unity. We deny every form of the principle of brute materialist utility, both on the individual level and also on the nation's. Beyond the nation we acknowledge eternal and immutable principles, in the name of which we should be ready to fight, to die, and to subordinate everything with at least the same determination as in the name of our right to live and defend our life. Truth and honour, for instance, are metaphysical prin-ciples, which we place much higher than our nation.'

We learned that the ascetic character of the Iron Guard movement is not generic, but concrete and, so to speak, observant. For instance, there is a fasting rule. Three days a week, about 800,000 men practice the so-called 'black fast', that is, abstention from every form of food,

drink, and tobacco. Prayer plays an equally important role in the movement. More than this, there is a rule of celibacy for the select Assault
Corps that bears the name of the two legionary leaders fallen in Spain,
Mota and Marin.[51] We ask Codreanu to tell us the precise meaning of
all this. He seems to concentrate a moment and then answers:

'There are two aspects. To explain them we need to bear in mind
the dualism of the human being, composed of a material, naturalistic
element and a spiritual one. When the first dominates the second, this
is "Hell". Every equilibrium between the two is precarious and contingent. Only the absolute dominion of the spirit over the body is the
normal condition and presupposition of every true force and every
true heroism. We practice fasting because it favours this condition, it
loosens the bonds of the body, and it favours the self-liberation and
self-affirmation of the pure will. When we add prayer to fasting, we ask
that powers from above unite with ours and sustain us invisibly. This
leads to the second aspect. It is a superstition to think that in every
combat, only material and simply human forces are decisive. No! In
combat there are also invisible and spiritual forces in play which are at
least as effective as the bodily ones. We are aware of the effectiveness
and importance of these forces. This is why we give a precise ascetic
character to the legionary movement. The principle of chastity was
also in force in the ancient chivalric orders. I emphasise, however, that
with us it is restricted to the Assault Corps, a restriction based on a
practical rationale, which is that for men who must devote themselves
completely to combat and not fear death, it is just as well that they do
not have the impediments of a family. Anyhow, men stay in this Corps
only until the end of their thirtieth year. In any case, however, there
still remains a commitment to principle. There are, on the one hand,
men who acknowledge only "life" and therefore seek only prosperity,

---

51   Legionaries Ion Mota and Vasile Marin went to Spain in 1936 to fight for Franco's nationalists in the Spanish
     Civil War. They were both killed in battle in January 1937.—Ed.

wealth, affluence, and opulence. On the other hand, there are men who aspire to something more than life, to glory and victory in a struggle that takes place within and without. The Iron Guard belong to this second group. Their warrior asceticism is completed with a second norm: a vow of poverty to which the elite of the movement's heads are pledged. They are called to renounce luxury, empty amusement, and so-called worldly distractions; in a word, an invitation to a true change of life that we extend to every legionnaire.'

Corporation and Roman Fidelity

(April–May 1938)

I t is curious that a nation in tune with a sane synthesis between renovation and tradition, like Fascist Italy, should have greeted the new German legislation concerning work with comments that frequently demonstrate a rather singular uncertainty of principles. This is the case, for instance, with old criticisms regarding the Nazi rules for labour. They resort to commonplaces, which we thought were long since relegated to the junkyards, derived from positivism and illuminist rationalism, denouncing this law as displaying a 'feudal' and 'medieval' mentality, accusing it of a repudiation of the 'successes won by the proletariat in a century of socialist struggles', and so on.

Naturally, for every sensible person, all this is immediately turned upside down into praise, and compels us to emphasise what is positive and 'traditional' in the new system from our point of view. And we can really speak of 'traditional'. In fact, those who attack the German corporative conception fail to notice that they are attacking their own spirit at the same time, not only in our common medieval tradition, but also the Roman corporative conception beyond this, in the name of ideological remnants that are creatures of modern decadence.

The new German labour law intends to reconstruct that productive solidarity which has been damaged by the Marxist ideology of class struggle, by scompletely suppressing that ideology and equally leaping over the union experience, both class-based and egalitarian, while harking back, *in primis et ante omnia*, to a Germanic ethical principle: the principle of fidelity and its counterpart, the principle of honour. The proprietor of the business is the head (literally, *Duce*, *Führer*), the blue and white collar workers are his followers (*Gefolgschaft*). Between the two is an advisory general staff: the 'council of trust' (*Vertrauungsrat*). There is no collective contract and no general corpus of corporative and union statutes on labour relations. The understanding is direct and occurs, case by case, between people, and before people within individual productive businesses. When the commitment of fidelity is violated, recourse is left to state labour trustees and the '*Honour Courts*'.

Semi-autarchic, ethically purified and reinforced, with an almost military structure, the individual businesses therefore absorb the economic momentum of the nation. They are not confused with the state, which, even while controlling them, remains on a level that is essentially superior to that of the economy.

The real merit of the initiative expressed by this new legislation is the resumption of the spirit of the best aspects of the Middle Ages, while rejecting — even if not yet radically — the prevarications, contaminations, and material reforms occurring in the economy of the plebs and the bourgeois coalitions.

The affirmation of the primacy of a spiritual and personalised principle — the principle of fidelity — in respect to every utilitarian, collectivist, and abstract relationship, has always characterised traditional organisations and, in particular, traditional corporations. The honour of one's own corporation, the pride in exercising the activity appropriate to it and the almost military solidarity, which is felt and willed, and for which the workman appears almost as a soldier, and the boss as an officer, in an enterprise to which both are committed, constitute the solid but immaterial bases of the professional unities of the Middle Ages.

For what concerns the ancient Roman culture, the time and cult of a particular divinity or 'hero' was the real centre, from which the unity and real life of the professional corporations began. Their constitution reproduced the virile and military constitution that belonged to the *gens*[52] and the patrician family. The mass of *sodales*[53] was called *populus*[54] and *ordo*[55] and was divided into centuries and decuries,[56] like the army and the people in solemn assemblies. Every century of the corporation had its own head, or centurion, and a lieutenant, *optio*, as in the legions. To be distinguished from the heads, the other members bore the name of *caligati* or *milites caligati*, as simple soldiers. The *magister*, in addition to being the technical director of the Roman corporations and the priest of its sacred fire, was also the administrator of justice and the guardian of the customs and norms of the association.

This discussion leads us to talk about the principle of fidelity in general. It is just as well to remind people who believe they are seeing an especially German patrimony in this that in Rome this principle had such power that, personified in the figure of a goddess, *fides* was the object of one of the most ancient and lively cults. *Fides romana* — as it was called in prehistoric times — *alma fides, fides sancta, sacra, casta, incorrupta* — these were the later names. According to Livy, *fides* characterised the Roman in front of the 'barbarian' by opposing the law of unconditioned adherence to the sworn pact against the contingency of

---

52 *Gens* is Latin for clan. In ancient Roman society, members of a *gens* believed that they shared common ancestry. They were both patriarchal and patrilineal. In the Roman method of naming, an individual's second name was his *gens*.—Ed.

53 The plural form of *sodalitas*, which was a voluntary association.—Ed.

54 'People'.—Ed.

55 'Order'.—Ed.

56 In civilian life, a century was a group of one hundred men who, collectively, had one vote in the Roman Assembly; in the military, it was a unit of one hundred (sometimes fewer) men under the command of a Centurion. A decury consisted of ten men led by a decurio.—Ed.

those who take unstable 'fortune' as their norm. The power of this law among the ancients was very great. Servius[57] comments, *magna erat apud maiores cura Fidei*.[58] Cicero warns prophetically that with the fall of *fides*, *virtus* too falls: the custom, the inner dignity, and the people's force of greatness, This is why *fides* could have its own symbolic temple at Rome — *aedes fidei populi romani*[59] — at the royal peak of the city, the Capitol, next to the temple of the greatest god, Jupiter. This closeness holds a profound significance. As Zeus for the Hellenes, Mithra for the Iranians, and Indra for the Indians, so Jupiter — the Roman representation of a similar metaphysical principle — was the god of oaths and loyalty at Rome. As god of the bright sky, *Lucetius*, he was also the god of sworn covenants and of interior commitments that are virile, loyal, clear, and explicit. They talked of *Jovis fiducia*, so that *fides* received a religious chrism for the Roman.

Fides did not remain at the level of a generic ethical principle. It was enhanced according to a political and heroic significance correlative to the enhancing of the Roman reality itself. This is why the Senate could appear as a living temple of fidelity — *fidei templum* — that would gather around the goddess' temple on the Capitol at times. This is why the most typical emblem for *fides* was the standard and eagle of the legions, and fidelity could take the absolute form of the warriors' fidelity before the Emperor — *fides equitum, fides militum*.[60] Fidelity, victory, and even immortal life then appeared as concepts connected by a mysterious link. The most complete and suggestive synthesis concerning this, under the title of *fides militum*, was given by a picture of the imperial epoch, where *fides*, personified and divinised, carries, among other things, a statue of victory and a globe topped by a

---

57   Maurus Servius Honoratus was a grammarian from the fourth and fifth centuries who is most noted for his commentaries on Virgil.—Ed.

58   Latin: 'Our ancestors had great concern for Good Faith.'—Ed.

59   Latin: 'The Temple of the Good Faith of the Roman People'.—Ed.

60   Latin: 'the fidelity of the knights, the fidelity of the soldiers'.—Ed.

phoenix, that is, the animal that symbolises resurrection, while on the other side there is an emperor sacrificing to Jupiter and being crowned by Victory. In these symbols there is a truly prodigious intensity of meaning.

A similar tradition was revived with new energy in our Middle Ages. *Fides, Treue*, trust are mottos characteristic of this period and are applied to the corporative field, the feudal field, and to the relations of the individual political entities with the super-political authority of the Holy Roman Empire. Ancient Roman ethics here meets and is enhanced by a corresponding ethics that was already living in Nordic blood. 'Fidelity is stronger than fire' is the formula in the *Nibelungenlied* that consecrates a tragic affair where the commitment of the warrior's fidelity imposes itself irresistibly beyond that of blood or of life itself.

Granted this, it is a matter of undeniable value that today we are seeking to put these kinds of principles back, front and centre, in order to make a life less materialistic which has been 'socialised' and depersonalised, and even to animate and cure the dark affair that are material activities and of the economy in general.

For people who respond with the formula of 'anachronism' and have their hearts set on 'the triumphs of the proletariat' of socialist memory, today there are beautiful lands available apart from those of our tradition, where these 'triumphs' are preserved under the sign of the hammer and sickle, claimed and fully developed. Today we are particularly aware that restoring the Roman and German tradition of 'fidelity' to its full force — on every level — is a fundamental point of every action of restoration.

Fidelity is what cannot be bought or sold. It obeys a law and attaches itself to a necessity. Convenience can be calculated, but *fides* can only be established by the spontaneous act of a man who is capable of inner nobility.

Fides means *personality and hierarchy.* It is the true overcoming of everything that is anodyne service, mechanical order, vile conformism, routine, superstructure, and even violence. It contains a vivifying power of virile spirituality, a roman and fascist force. When it disappears, the tension of every organisation, every law, and every institution becomes a creature deprived of inner support, which will collapse at the first blow.

Party or Order?

(2 JANUARY 1940)

We have recently read some interesting considerations regarding the concept of 'party', which, in our opinion, deserve to be noticed and discussed because of their importance. This is especially true just now, when the amendments introduced by the Grand Council to the Fascist Party's constitution demonstrate that they are far from wanting to rest on the *status quo*, and instead that there is a lively need to revise the existing order and make it increasingly coherent in relation to the spirit from which it arose. In fact, Roberto Farinacci has emphasised that these amendments, 'although they might appear to be a retreat at first glance, are in reality an expansion and strengthening'. The cornerstone of every organisation is established by the principle of greatest spiritual centralisation and the greatest administrative decentralisation. This very principle is the animating spirit behind the recent reform. Through it, the Fascist Party is going to adjust itself more consistently with its mission, 'which is to be the lively animator and disciplining energy of everything and everybody. For this, it is necessary that this energy not be dissipated and nearly submerged in the vast network of numerous organisations, but concentrated in itself, ready for and capable of any action'.

Today there is, therefore, a reconfirmation of the cure which accentuates those aspects of the Party by means of which they constitute a type of soul — speaking like an Aristotelian, we could say, a type of *entelechia*, the formative and animating vital principle — for the new state. What further developments are theoretically conceivable in such a direction?

The first aspect we want to treat is connected to a question that, superficially considered, might seem to be merely one of names. We are dealing with the designation of 'party', a term which originated from the world of parliamentary democracy and has become absolutely self-contradictory where there is a single party that has assumed the authority of the state and has declared every other party illegal. It is curious that in the eighteen years of the new regime, no one has ever thought to propose the substitution of this word with an original term that fits reality better. A different designation would fit the functions and effective significance of the Fascist Party more effectively: that of Order. For this designation we do not refer to the communities of a properly religious or monastic type, but especially to the ancient chivalric organisations. The idea of Order will then correspond to that of an elite and a voluntary formation with 'ascetic' and militant traits, which essentially defends an idea preserving principles and a tradition, and works to support a given community of persons, who are more numerous, but less qualified, more dedicated to particular and contingent interests, and less penetrated by a sentiment of high political and ethical responsibility.

In reality, a name like, for example, the *Fascist Order of the Italian Empire* would not be inferior in dignity to the present name, 'National Fascist Party', and as symbol, myth, or force-idea, the substitution would be advantageous. With the new name, the old order of ideas of demo-liberal party government would be definitively excluded as even the echo of a name, and it would be a manifestation of the same tendency that has led logically to the recent suppression of the names 'parliament' and 'deputy'.

This 'liturgy of power', which plays a far from negligible role in every authoritarian and traditional political order, would receive a precise and significant advancement by moving from Party to Order. The new name would always bring to mind the task of defending the Party from every bureaucratisation and against the return of bourgeois elements, always emphasising the 'sacred' side of the commitment that it assumes. This would serve to give a mediating role to its oath so that its members would have no other alternative besides fidelity or treason in respect to the principles of its own internal forum, which would be superior to, rather than answerable to, any external authority or control. If there is a power hidden in every word, as in the ancient view, we have no doubt that the designation of 'order' would be the most appropriate one to evoke the necessary forces for the highest revolutionary vocation and for a definitive abolition of the so-called 'modern' conception of the state; that is, the state as a rationalistic, mechanical, and agnostic entity, like the 'rule of law' or the 'police state' or the 'economic state' of earlier ideologies.

If we analyse the processes that have contributed the most to the crisis of modern society and civilisation, we find first of all the separation of spiritual authority from temporal power, or the political element. This separation has been followed by a real inversion. In the course of drawing its highest significance and real legitimacy from reference to a spiritual reality, the political element has positioned itself as *ultima ratio*[61] and had tried to subordinate the spiritual authority to itself, while offering none but 'realistic' motives of utility or opportunism as the basis for its right and new pretensions — at most a brute will to power. We need to be very conscious that it is impossible to speak seriously of a revival or reconstruction before restoring the hierarchical values that belong to every normal and traditional order. This vocation is contained in the highest potentialities of the Fascist revolution. The

---

61   Latin: 'the last word'.—Ed.

starting point of the new Fascist political idea is neither an abstractly juridical principle nor a material reality, but rather a new worldview that is suffused with spiritual meanings. Right after worldview there comes the ideal of a given human type, the ideal of 'Mussolini's man' understood in these terms so that it can be the basis and reference point for the formation of a new kind of 'race of the spirit', with its own very precise countenance and 'style'. In third place comes Fascism as life and concrete actualisation of the aforesaid general consideration and human ideal in a precise organisation, which in these terms, in the logic of a restorative process so conceived, will have less the traits of the 'Party' than those of an Order. In the Party as Fascist Order of the Italian Empire the new, spiritually revolutionary idea would be incarnated, the evocation of the deepest forces of the race will be consummated, a 'tradition' will be preserved and transmitted, and there will be the definitive achievement of the type of a virile, implacable organisation. This organisation will be formed less from 'men of a party' and simple 'card-carrying' Party members, adherents of a given political programme for reasons of opportunism and utility, but rather by spirits united in a unique vocation with spiritual traits, more sacred than profane, and by a life rigidly inspired by ethical principles and motives that are more than individual.

This appears to us to be the context of a Fascist revolutionary radicalism, a complete political transformation, a definitive coherent alignment of forces, and values according to which Mussolini's Italy is and can always continue to be at the head of every possible movement of reconstruction in the West.

The Spiritual Bases of the Japanese Imperial Idea

(November–December 1940)

The signing of the Anti-Comintern Pact (6 November 1937) and the Tripartite Pact (27 September 1940) by Italy, Germany, and Japan provided occasions to emphasise the common political interests they presupposed. Almost no one, however, thought to discuss them from the perspective of worldview, spirituality, or traditional principles in order to see to what extent there was also a certain convergence here. On the contrary, to most people this assumption seemed absurd. Most people consider Japan another world, which will always remain closed to our mentality. People believe that its state and its tradition are the result of a mentality that no bridge can connect to Western man's way of thinking. To a large extent this is a mistake. It is an opinion that can be true only from an empiricist viewpoint, the viewpoint of people who believe that nothing exists beyond what is conditioned by the naturalistic element, whether geographic, ethnic, or racist in the narrow sense. Wherever there exists a 'traditional' culture in the highest sense of this term, there is always something superior to all this, something potentially universal, which in its diverse elements reveals the different expressions of a unique content. Japan is among the most traditional cultures that still exist. If a lack of understanding exists between some Western cultures and the Japanese, the cause does not proceed so much from a difference of race as from the fact that the latter — the Western cultures — find themselves outside of Tradition, that is, they are the product of a 'profane' and anti-traditional spirit, a situation which puts them in opposition not only to Eastern cultures, but also to every normal and higher culture of our own Western past.

It is in fact essential to acknowledge that, even if it does so in forms appropriate for a different race and environment, Japan still firmly defends values today that the West, in the contingencies of its history, has lost and can only hope to regain in future developments stemming from restorative revolutions. On this terrain there can well be a convergence. By representing an open challenge to every 'evolved' and 'modern' political ideology, by holding firmly to transcendent and anti-secular significance, even in the political and governmental order, Japan can in a certain way work for us as a type of reagent, can help us to overcome compromises imposed by necessity, and can spur our spiritual courage, and point out to us new paths to the summit. Similarly, we find it useful to hint at the Japanese political idea, which is only superficially known to most people.

The political and national ideal of Japan — *Ymato damashii* — can be summed up in calling the imperial tradition 'divine'. 'Following the command, I shall descend from heaven', the patriarch of the Japanese sovereigns says in the *Ko-ji-ki*, the chief text of Japanese tradition. These sovereigns are not considered human beings. They form a unity with the solar goddess Amaterasu Omikami, on the basis of an archaic and uninterrupted dynastic and spiritual tradition, but even historically the Japanese dynasty has a continuity of over two thousand years. Here the act of governing and ruling is united with cult. It is at one and the same time a rite, a religious act. The word *matsurigoto* means both government in the strict sense, that is, temporal power, and cult, the 'exercise of religious things'. This ambiguity is full of significance, because it refers to the unbreakable synthesis between spiritual authority and temporal power in a single person, a synthesis that belongs to all primordial traditional cultures, including Rome.

Japan is therefore the only contemporary state that finds itself in the happy condition of knowing nothing of the problem of the reconciliation between the national and racial idea and the religious idea. In Japan, religion is politics and politics is religion. The Japanese religion, Shintoism, has *ciughi* as its cornerstone — that is, absolute fidelity to the Emperor, the exact equivalent of what was *fides* in the Roman and Germanic Ghibelline Middle Ages and to a certain degree in ancient Rome. The religious duty is also dissolved into fidelity before the state, because in Japan the state is not a human creation, but has a divine basis and at its centre there is a being that is more than a man, even if — as the texts inform us — it does not have the character of an absolute God of the monotheistic type.

Since this is the only reference point for the piety of the individual, the result is that every virtue or act of this individual or collective life ends with justifying itself in terms of *fides*, transcendent fidelity to the Chief: *ciughi*. Fidelity and loyalty in Japan are therefore concepts that are valid not only in the warrior and chivalric sphere, but include respect for parents, solidarity between relatives or friends, the practice of virtue, respect for the laws, harmony between spouses with a proper hierarchical relationship between the sexes, productivity in the field of industry and the economy, work and study, the task of forming one's own character, and the defence of blood and race. All this is 'fidelity' and, in the last instance, fidelity before the Sovereign. Every antisocial, immoral, and criminal act on this basis does not signify the transgression of an abstract norm, a more or less anodyne or conventional 'social' law. No! It is treason, disloyalty, and ignominy comparable to what rebounds on a warrior who deserts his post or betrays the commitment covenanted by him in a manly fashion with his chief. They are therefore not 'criminals', but rather 'traitors', beings incapable of honour.

It is interesting to notice that this kind of view, which is still alive and well in Japan, reflects what every other traditional culture, of East and West, originally knew, but then lost. It is now reappearing again in Fascism and National Socialism. In these movements, too, there is a growing tendency to give a basis that is ethical and virile, and therefore anti-positivist, to the notion of the rule of law, of social morality, and moreover of liability and responsibility. However, unlike Japan, in our country we do not have the supreme, religious reference point, which is established in Japanese tradition through the supernatural character of the imperial function.

The Japanese sovereign possesses this character, even more than for his descent, which is considered non-human and, as we mentioned, reaches back to prehistoric epochs, and also because of the 'Triple Treasure — *Sanshu no Jingi* — emblems of divine power: mirror, pearl, and sword. There is no coronation or investiture ceremony in Japan. The new sovereign becomes Emperor when he assumes the Triple Treasure, an act that marks and seals his right from above. The traditions that refer to this are so ancient that their original meaning survives only in a fragmentary and unclear form, even in Japan itself. What should we really think, for instance, about the relationship that exists between the sovereign and the female divinity of the Sun? It is not easy to deal here with a problem like this one, which, anyhow, we have already discussed elsewhere. We shall only say that the physical Sun functions here as a symbol for a spiritual reality by means of a transcendent 'solarity'. The fact that this force is conceived of as being female could probably be explained like many heroic myths, where symbolic women, queens, or female divinities play a significant role and lead beings who are especially gifted and tested to the regal function. This symbolism means that, in respect to spiritual, celestial, and 'solar' power, the sovereign, by assuming this function and maintaining himself also as a 'man', has to preserve the affirmative and supremely royal quality that man has before woman in every normal relationship. This is precisely the opposite of the Semitic attitude of servility before the divine.

The relationship of 'identity', moreover, is emphasised by the first object of the imperial Triple Treasure, the mirror, which is called *Yata no Kagami*, that is, august spirit. There is a 'solar' force in this as in a magic 'presence'. Therefore the mirror invites the sovereign to acknowledge his true image, that is, to be always aware of his identity in relation to the solar force.

There are two aspects to consider about the second symbol, the sword. The first, exoteric one, corresponds more or less to the meaning that the sword has had everywhere as an emblem of the temporal power. Moreover, in Japan it is a reference to the ability to discriminate between good and evil, real and unreal, so as to be able to be a just judge on Earth. Nonetheless, the second aspect of the symbolism in question — a more secret and esoteric aspect — will give a sort of metaphysical foundation to this ability. The myth in fact says that the sword was originally brandished to 'kill the dragon with eight heads' of the brother of the solar goddess. We cannot deal here with the symbolism of this event and of the number 'eight' that occurs therein. We shall only say that again, there is a reference to a supernatural achievement, which presupposes the destruction of lower, 'telluric' influences on different levels of conditioned existence.

As for the symbol of the stone, or pearl of stone, *tama*, from the outer viewpoint it refers to Buddhism, which knows the mystic pearl of 'compassion', in the highest sense of understanding, of human sentiment, of greatness and openness of mind — in Sanskrit, *mahâtmâ*. The Japanese word *tama*, however, also means 'soul' or 'divinity', and the symbolism of the 'celestial stone' effectively takes us rather far back in time. The Grail itself in Wolfram von Eschenbach's text appears as a divine or celestial stone — *lapis ex coelo* — closely connected to the idea of transcendent kingdom, while the ancient English tradition knows the so-called 'stone of destiny' — *Lia Fáil* — which has played a part in the consecration of legitimate kings since prehistoric times. We could easily find many more similar references. In general a sacred stone appears everywhere a centre is established of a 'traditional' organisation in the higher sense, that is, almost in the sense of a 'world centre'. We can recall the *omphalos* of Delphi and even the papal allegory of Peter as 'rock' (*pietra*) in the Gospels.

As we said, the transcendent nature of sovereignty, marked with these symbols of the triple treasure, constitutes the cornerstone of the entire Japanese doctrine of Empire and is still valid as dogma. These words are part of the commentary of Prince Ito Hirobumi[62] on the Japanese constitution: 'The sacred throne was created when the Earth parted from the sky (i.e., as a sort of surrogate for the degeneration of an existing primordial unity of the terrestrial and the divine). The sovereign descends from heaven and is divine and sacred.' In the official text *Kokutai no Hongi* that was recently published (1937) by the Japanese Ministry of National Education,[63] the same idea is found, but in a yet more radical formulation. We shall report some points in Marenga's translation: 'The sovereigns of Japan descend from a solar goddess. Japan has always been ruled by a single dynasty. It is a unique country in the world, without peers. The goddess is present in the imperial mirror of the temple of Ise.[64] The three symbols of power have

---

62   Prince Ito Hirobumi (1841–1909) was a samurai and also served as Prime Minister of Japan on four occasions. He spent 18 months studying the constitutional systems of Europe, accepting and rejecting some of their ideas for Japan, and was instrumental in the creation of the Meiji Constitution, which restored direct power to the Emperor at the same time that it established many democratic institutions. He was assassinated by a Korean nationalist.—Ed.

63   *Kokutai no Hongi: Cardinal Principles of the National Entity of Japan* (Cambridge: Harvard University Press, 1949).—Ed.

64   The Grand Shrine at Ise is a temple complex which is one of the most important in Shintoism, and is of great importance to the Japanese imperial family, which is responsible for its maintenance.—Ed.

been delivered by the goddess. The rule of the empire is divine. The sovereigns are visible divinities. They are different from the rulers of any other nation, because they are not chosen by the people. The act of governing the nation is identical to that of paying homage to the gods according to the Shinto rites. The sovereign is the people. They are the same thing. Loyalty to the sovereign is the basis of all morality.' All this is the official ideology of the state; it is the basis of the particular national sentiment; it is the foundation of the ideals and virtues of every Japanese; it is the weapon used to fight materialism, individualism, collectivism, and especially Bolshevism, which is correctly considered as the extreme antithesis of the Japanese political idea. It is the deep source of every heroic act and every sacrifice; it is the faith, the soul of the Yamato[65] race. In 1935, Professor Minobe made himself leader of an attempt at 'Enlightenment' reform. He wanted to make of the throne a simple branch of the government, and therefore to 'constitutionalise' and 'positivise' the institution of the monarchy. This unleashed a most violent reaction in the soul of the Japanese and especially in the army.[66] The divine nature and origin of the sovereign was once again solemnly affirmed.

The principle according to which the sovereign is the people has an almost racial basis. The dynasty is considered as the original stock from which arise or derive the principal lines of the Japanese race. Thus, the nation is conceived as a single large family or *gens*[67] in the ancient sense. This myth cements the pride and solidarity that racism seeks to arouse in us today, since it gives an almost patriarchal hue to

---

65 Yamato is the ancient name for the largest ethnic group of native Japanese.—Ed.

66 Tatsukichi Minobe (1873–1948) was a law professor who specialised in constitutional law. Although his interpretations were widely accepted, including by the Emperor himself, for many years, by 1935 he was accused of being a traitor by those military officers and nationalists who wished to see the Emperor vested with absolute power. He was forced to resign and his works were discredited and banned. After the war, however, he participated in the creation of Japan's new constitution.—Ed.

67 *Gens* is Latin for clan. In ancient Roman society, members of a gens believed that they shared common ancestry. They were both patriarchal and patrilineal.—Ed.

Japanese loyalty. Loyalty on this foundation is almost *pietas*;[68] it is not exhausted in the free act of the individual, it is a duty of the blood. Naturally, this sentiment is especially alive among the elements closest to the imperial summit, that is, in the *bushi* or *samurai*, who constitute the warrior or feudal class, conceived as the flower of Japanese society according to the ancient proverb: 'What the cherry is among blossoms, so is the *bushi* among men.' The organisation of the *samurai* or *bushi* into a true caste, in which the traits, between ascetic and military, of our ancient chivalric orders are precisely reflected, dates back to about 1,500 years ago. The doctrine that is their soul and law, the *bushido*, is, however, rather older, and harmonises with the idea of the Japanese state. As the foundation of precise ethical, social, spiritual, and even biological norms, it has been faithfully handed down from generation to generation to our own days. This caste is the jealous guardian of the tradition. Just as it is loyal unto death to the sovereign, it is equally so to the dogma of divine regality, which, today as in centuries past, it is ready to defend against any profanation and secularisation.

The doctrine of *bushido*, like the doctrine of the old Western chivalry, does not concern only the profession of arms (and so it would be a mistake to consider the *samurai* as a simple 'military caste'), but involves the entire tenor of life. It is way of being that essentially corresponds to a race of the spirit, beyond a race of blood. Aside from the supreme norm of loyalty, stronger than life or death, *bushido* contains the formation of the warrior, but in a special sense, which is hardly accessible to the contemporary European mentality, which easily confuses the warrior with the soldier and always associates it with the idea of something hard, rigid, and closed. An essential element of the 'way of the *bushi*', however, is an interiorising of heroism and force, the victory over one's own nature that is fundamental for 'refinement', nobility,

---

68 *Pietas*, to the ancient Romans, was the characteristic of absolute devotion and loyalty, both to one's community as well as in the religious sense.—Ed.

'style', and 'beauty' as all this is conceived in Japan. The *bushi*, therefore, is traditionally practiced in the domination of his own thoughts and sentiments, of his own intensiveness and passionate nature, until he reaches an asceticism that is *sui generis*.[69] Moreover, even today the *bushido* is not foreign to the practices and discipline of Zen, which is one of the most 'esoteric' schools of Buddhism, with its own methods of controlling and awakening deep human energies, which border on the occult, while always emphasising the demand that every material realisation — for instance, the profession of arms and the Japanese way of fighting, *jujutsu*[70] — be understood as symbol and foundation for a spiritual realisation. As on the one hand there is the strictest law of honour, the scrupulous care to avoid even the lightest stain casting a shadow on the family to which the *samurai* belongs, so on the other hand there is the ideal of a subtle, inflexible, and unfathomable force of dominion which flees any theatrical and narcissistic exhibition, and any vanity, and recalls the teaching of Lao Tzu about the action that is not material action, *wei-wu-wei*,[71] and because of its invisibility is irresistible.

People in Italy who seriously defend the idea of a 'total education', especially with reference to the problem of future elites, cannot view these aspects of Japanese culture with indifference. They should rather acknowledge that the West, for centuries now, using the excuse of dominating nature and matter, has almost completely abandoned the task of ruling themselves; that in the West serious mistakes often subsist about what manliness really means, which is unilaterally confused with its coarsest, muscular, or violently 'voluntarist' forms; that because of unfortunate circumstances, the asceticism that has been

---

69 Latin: 'in a class by itself'.—Ed.

70 A form of martial arts.—Ed.

71 In Buddhism, *wei-wu-wei* designates a way of acting and being that is in complete harmony with the surrounding world, so as not to resist it or attempt to change it in any way. In Taoism this is regarded as the highest form of action.—Ed.

acknowledged most especially in the West is asceticism of the religious type that is self-abnegating and contemplative, not the asceticism that can integrate, enhance, and transform a warrior vocation and an aristocratic ethics. To the degree to which there is a serious intention to overcome all these limitations with a truly integral virile education, ideas very close to those of *bushido* seem to us far from foreign and extraneous, but instead present a special character of relevance for the spiritual vanguard of our own movements of restoration.

Finally, a last point. Starting from the centre, which is constituted by the dynasty and radiating outward through veins constituted by the great *bushi* families, the transcendent conception of the Japanese state will reach all the remaining elements of the nation and then, step by step, permeate the entire national society with the same meaning. All Japan therefore feels itself as the bearer of a divine force and as a unique race, which has a universal mission that is irreducible to any demand of what is only material. This is not an old, obsolete faith. Among the verses that every Japanese student learns in today's schools from a tender age are found, for instance, the following: 'Japan is the only divine land. The Japanese people are the only divine people, and therefore Japan can be the light of the world.' The well-known politician, Yosuke Matsuoka,[72] who recently represented his country at the League of Nations, expressed himself as follows: 'I am convinced that the mission of the Yamato race (i.e., the Japanese) is to protect the human race from hell, to safeguard it from destruction, and to lead it to a world of clarity.'

Here we ourselves face a 'myth', a force-idea, intended to create a high degree of tension in a people. As Rudolf Walter has mentioned, the notion of a 'chosen people' and a super-national mission are in reality very far from constituting a solely Japanese patrimony. The

---

72   Yosuke Matsuoka (1880–1946) was a Japanese diplomat, and later Minister of Foreign Affairs for Imperial Japan during 1940–41. As the head of the Japanese delegation to the League of Nations in 1933, his speech was followed by a walkout that announced Japan's withdrawal from the League.—Ed.

same sentiment is found wherever a people has been pervaded by a metaphysical sense through which, behind the human forces that belong to it, forces from on high are also acting. Thus we are dealing with a faith that the Aryan races also possessed, and, if we want to find an equivalent in the West no less august than the Japanese for antiquity, we need only remember the Roman symbol, the secular faith in *aeternitas Romae*[73] and the super-national and universal mission of the Roman race.

Today, these correspondences do not lack a precise meaning. Once the most contingent part of Japanese ideology, its exclusivism, has been separated, what remains as its central nucleus is the idea of a struggle that is justified not only by ambitions of material power and political reason, but also by an idea, a mission, and a vocation of spiritual dominion, and basically by a transcendent reference point. In one form or another, insights of this sort are being affirmed with increasing clarity in the struggle being fought today to limit the power of other myths and vocations. Japan can find itself with us, and especially with the conscious advocates of the Roman imperial tradition, on the same front, which is not only political, material, and military, but also spiritual and ideal. The ethnic and naturalistic differences here cannot mask the undeniable convergence in the theme of the traditional spirit except to the eyes of the myopic. Those who knew how to preserve this spirit from remote epochs can join together to fight beside those who are today trying to reconquer it after having overcome the decadence, disintegration, and darkness that has characterised the pseudo-civilisation of the modern world.

---

73   Literally 'eternal Rome', the concept was promulgated by Saint Augustine in his *City of God*, based on a pre-Christian Roman doctrine, that Rome is the apex of civilisation which stands first among the world's peoples.—Ed.

Scientific Racism's Mistake

(1942)

The debate on racism has recently been revived. This has stemmed less from a sincere desire to contribute to an objective clarification of the problems, however, than from the ambitions of certain groups. In it, a false note has been sounded that should be pointed out. We are referring to people who today insist on 'scientific racism'. They never tire of repeating that the problem of race should be expressed in terms that are 'purely scientific' and biological, and have chosen as a false target an undefined 'spiritual racism', against which they fight like Don Quixote against the windmills.

Here we have a misunderstanding that needs to be cleared up; cleared up, of course, before a public in good faith, and not before those who created it — people who almost always know perfectly well what the real situation is, but who are the first not to believe what they say. The relevant explanation is necessary because we are dealing essentially with intellectual integrity and honesty. When writers fail to demonstrate these elementary qualities of character, we think it is futile for them to proclaim themselves racists and to boast of their Aryan body type, which could even be quite true, and thus make themselves out as ready to eat Jews alive. We just used the term 'false note'. There is no other way to characterise the fact that, in a climate replete with spiritual, ethical, and heroic forces such as Fascism's, they make use of the superstition of 'scientism' in order to make an impression on the naïve. They have nothing but the idol of 'science' at their disposal, a fetish belonging to the toolbox of the age of democracy and the Enlightenment, and of the more or less Masonic and rationalist progressivism of the nineteenth century. This is really 'speaking the people's language', but in the worst sense of the expression.

Ideologies, which the more serious culture of a country has surpassed, often survive for a long time by the force of inertia in the less cultivated levels of a nation. We know well the drunken rampages of the 'Enlightenment' and its Jacobin consequences. People no longer believed in God, tradition, or blood, but only in Science with a capital S. Only with Science — and by this they naturally meant materialist and 'positivistic' science — would begin the age of truth and certainty, and the obscurantism and superstition of earlier times would be overcome. Science would create prosperity and happiness for humanity. The more extreme forms of these ideological aberrations think that the peoples will be led into the future not, of course, by dynastic, spiritual, or heroic aristocracies, but by groups of technicians and scientists. According to this kind of radicalism, these progressivist and Enlightenment ideas have long since disappeared. Only Bolshevism is silly enough to believe that science and technology will open the doors of a new earthly paradise to the depersonalised and materialised masses.

Remnants of this same mentality, however, survive in less educated circles. The superstition of 'science' survives. People have been persuaded that it is only with science that we 'get serious'; that only science imposes itself on everyone with the language of facts, offers precise certainties, and establishes solid knowledge. They believe that everything else is fog and arbitrary ideas, more or less as Marxism calls everything that transcends the level of the brute economy 'superstructure'. Anyway, people who today are agitating so loudly for a 'purely scientific racism' are absolutely 'speaking the people's language'. Instead of helping to liquidate these remnants of an obsolete myth that survive in the less educated classes, they repeat them as a solid basis for 'making an impression', and to confer a false authority by means that are authoritative in their exterior affirmations, but which are incoherent and confused before every serious investigation conducted with sound thought. If we were dealing here with the natural sciences on a purely physical or abstractly classificatory level, the evil would not be fundamentally serious. In this field it is not possible to correct overnight mental deformations that date back centuries, and to convince everyone that the modern 'scientific' knowledge of nature is a crippled and inorganic knowledge that concerns only one sector of reality and, indeed, the least interesting sector. What it calls 'facts' do not exist in themselves, but are the artificial products of an arbitrary abstraction, and acquire different meanings according to the system which is used to interpret them. In the modern critique of science, all this is a commonplace.

There is no need to consult a Boutroux,[74] a Guénon, a Pavese,[75] or a Poincaré.[76] Every honest scientist, if taken *in camera caritatis*,[77] will of course acknowledge the relativism and contingency of the modern scientific 'knowledge' of nature. The myth of its 'indisputable facts' and its indisputable certainty belongs only to the grossest forms of vulgarisation and are related to the ideological remnants of the 'Enlightenment' that we have already mentioned. Since, however, we are still far from

---

74 Émile Boutroux (1845–1921) was a French philosopher who held that modern science and religion could be reconciled. He was an adherent of the Theistic Personalist school, and not the later form of French Personalism which originated in which postulated that everything which exists must be understood as a manifestation of God, or the divine personality, and that, therefore, all individuals are an expression of a single, divine will.—Ed.

75 Roberto Pavese wrote several books on philosophy and parapsychology.—Ed.

76 Henri Poincaré (1854–1912) was a French mathematician and physicist who contributed to the development of the Theory of Relativity of Einstein. He was also known for his writings on the philosophy of science.—Ed.

77 Latin: figuratively, 'in secret'.—Ed.

the restoration of a traditional, qualitative, and living knowledge of nature, the illusions that befuddle the general public about the actual range of the physical sciences do not have great consequences. Matters begin to proceed differently when we are no longer dealing with the physical and classificatory sciences, but with the domain of life, that is, the biological sciences. Here the consequences of the scientistic superstition could be absolutely deleterious. It is precisely to this field that the persons to whom we are alluding refer dogmatically, when they proceed to claim that this legendary 'objectivity' exists in the field of biological science, this language of 'pure and indisputable facts', this *ipse dixit*,[78] that modern epistemology has denied even in the domain of the physical sciences. In the area of social applications it has provoked these words from Mussolini: 'There is nothing truly scientific in the world. Science explains the How of phenomena, but it does not explain their Why.'[79]

There is also a question here of a special ignorance. Because of a misunderstood patriotism, the people we are talking about, who proclaim scientific racism without, however, possessing any scientific competence, are basically referring to Italian biology and anthropology. Italian biology and anthropology are areas that do not, unfortunately, stand at the forefront in the overall context of world research because of the simple fact that they reflect the general climate, both materialist and positivist, of nineteenth century Italy. On the contrary, many recent currents in biology and genetics have been compelled to assume working hypotheses and criteria that lead rather far afield from 'positivism' and scientism, from the narrow confines in which

---

78   Latin: figuratively, meaning a statement made on no other authority other than the person making it.—Ed.

79   *Scritti e discorsi*, vol. II (Milan: Hoepli, 1934), p. 160.

they find themselves. It is enough to cite Driesch[80] and Dacque.[81] In the Italian circles we are discussing, all this counts as non-existent. The biology that they make into a myth is essentially an outdated biology in the field of technical scientific research. They probably do not know this. Even if they did know it, it would probably change nothing, because for them it is not a question of explaining and working through the truth, but rather of spreading simple propaganda in a mistaken direction. And why is this? If we leave aside personal interests, it is essentially from fear. These people are well aware that, whenever the problem of race has not been discussed on a simply 'scientific' and 'biological' level, but rather in a totalitarian fashion, as happens in Germany, serious difficulties have arisen. We run into various tendencies, and headaches and complications are created, which, despite the outward appearance of polemical activism, they very much prefer to offer easy lies about, sparing the 'headaches'. These people do not notice that they are abdicating and playing the enemy's game. In fact, what more could those who would like to monopolise spiritual values, everything that is 'tradition' and worldview, ask for than to limit the problem of race to the material, biological, and 'scientific' level so as to have a free hand before such a castrated racism? The scientistic direction of racist propaganda is mistaken, because if the idea of race is really to become a force in Italy, it must be understood *in primis et ante omnia*[82] in the ethical and political field as spiritual and heroic. All the rest could only be working out the details.

---

80 Hans Driesch (1867–1941) was a German biologist and philosopher who successfully produced the first clone of an animal, a sea urchin, in 1891. He developed a philosophy called entelechy, denoting the existence of a psychic life-force that drives and permeates all life.—Ed.

81 Edgar Dacqué (1878–1945) was a German paleontologist and Theosophist. He sought to combine his scientific and mystical beliefs, postulating such ideas as racial memory that gave humans a memory of their experiences from previous stages of evolution, and that forms of life were self-evolving and were attempting to attain their most perfect development.—Ed.

82 Latin: 'first and foremost'.—Ed.

This consideration is not only the indispensable premise for coherence between the racist idea and Fascist ideals, but is also the necessary condition to avoid a series of absurdities that are obvious. For instance, the people we are discussing hold the myth of the 'Italian race' dear. It is well-known that from the scientific and purely biological point of view, an Italian race does not exist. The biological and anthropological races are unities that have nothing to do with the historic nations, in which more or less all races are found, distributed in different ways. And so we would end up with a result that is quite the opposite of the solidarity at which these people are confusedly aiming, by talking improperly and unscientifically of an 'Italian race'. If, then, there is no common race on the biological and anthropological level, on what basis can we 'scientifically' found a myth like the one to which we have just referred? The theory of internal races, or races of the soul, which might come to our aid here, is exactly what has the effect of a thorn in the side of the people we are talking about — for mysterious reasons that will end by becoming clear. And on the purely scientific, biological, and anthropological level, what about the Jewish problem? Do they not notice the absurdity of insisting on dealing exclusively with it from the purely scientific point of view, while the Jewish problem in Italy has been imposed not on a biological basis, but on an essentially political and spiritual one? The banning of Jews from public life in Italy did not take place because their lips and noses and cranial indices were actually radically different from those of some 'Mediterranid' racial components, which are also present in our people. It happened rather on the basis of their works, their lifestyle and actions, and their spirit. Anyhow, from the 'purely anthropological' point of view, I find talk of a 'Hebrew race' rather risky. It is well-known that modern Israel does not constitute a race according to the prevalent opinion in modern racism, but rather a people comprised of rather diverse racial components.

Another point: on a 'purely biological' and positivist scientific basis, even the means of individuating the unity of Israel would be lacking. It is, however, very real, but it is found on a rather different level. This is why Roberto Farinacci has correctly written, 'Is it really necessary to justify our racism by resorting to differences in hair or noses, of hands and feet? Is it really necessary to entrust to analyses of blood and chromosomes what is a question of a political and spiritual nature? Of course not! We can follow a more certain path, which does not admit debates and removes every doubt, and persuades the most stubborn. We do not need the anthropologist and the biologist to prove that we belong to a different race.' (*Vita Italiana*, July 1942) Farinacci is expressing what is immediately acknowledged by people who really feel the problem of race, but not by those who squeal about it because it suits them or because they have received their marching orders. If race is not experienced directly as a way of being and a spontaneous interior realty, dolls from an anthropological museum, cranial measurements, and racial laws will be of very little use.

Of course human beings also have bodies, but research conducted on bodily, somatic, and anthropological phenomena is conclusive and serious only when these phenomena can count as signs and symptoms of a corresponding interior reality, and after centuries of crossbreeding this does not always happen. Only by acknowledging this frankly and openly, and leaving behind once and for all the scientific myth, is it possible to speak the people's language — now in the good sense of the expression — and to prepare in Italy, little by little, a reawakening of an Aryan racial consciousness. Since it is useless to hide the fact: especially today, it is the Italian people who are wondering whether, finally, Jews are not becoming a kind of scapegoat, since they see everywhere one hundred percent 'Aryan' types who brazenly hoard, force prices up and take unfair profits, social climbers, and — why not? — even journalists who do not hesitate to resort to the most twisted and unfair methods for polemical purposes.

Let us add that if today there is so much talk of race, the reason is that people have finally noticed the fact of our effective decadence in Europe. Where race was really alive and strong, no one talked about it. A secure instinct sufficed as a guide. This instinct silently conferred an unwritten authority with very precise norms and laws. Scientific racism is following the wrong path, because it almost wants to repeat the attempt to create the homunculus. It seriously believes (or at least lets it be understood) that, when race is in trouble, it can be reconstructed and rescued, as it were, with laboratory procedures on the basis of 'positive' acquired knowledge, almost as how artificial mushrooms are grown when there is a shortage of natural ones. The undoubted and integral sentiment of race and blood which is found in the ancient Aryan cultures of the East such as Sparta, the old Roman aristocracy, and certain parts of Europe's nobility, did not need these shenanigans. It was secure without these pseudo-scientific excuses, which, let us say it once more, can make an impression only on the rabble and rustics of the world of our middle class and intellectuals. Awakening the sentiment and dignity of race directly, by essentially spiritual means, is what really matters. Biology, genetics, anthropology, Mendelian laws, and whatever else you may desire are all useful things, but are subordinate, like accessory tools and sources of knowledge to be used *cum grano salis*,[83] while always being aware of the demands of a superior ethical and political character. This is to say, there must be an integral conception of race, one that is especially ethical and spiritual in order to fix the measure and means by which certain scientific 'knowledge' can be accepted and incorporated as auxiliary elements. Here the contributions will never be very many, because, as we have said, biology and anthropology bear birth defects, always and indelibly. This is to

---

83   Latin: 'with a grain of salt'.—Ed.

say, they are founded on premises of a materialist and evolutionary character which are incompatible with what is needed for any truly superior sentiment of race.

We wonder, in fact, what will come of a sentiment taken from disciplines in which people continue to seriously believe in man's having descended from the monkey, more or less implicitly, and where, with the predominance of the theory of a single origin for life, it is necessary to resort to a materialistic determinism. Otherwise they may have recourse to the miraculous idea of 'scientifically' inexplicable mutations, in order to 'explain' the differentiation of species and races from one hypothetical homogenous original substance. Try to touch similar scientistic superstitions, or try to recall the testimony of all ancient peoples concerning the earliest races, which were not animals but almost 'divine', and you will suddenly see yourself accused of an anti-scientific mentality and even of…magic. This is exactly the charge levelled at us by Canella,[84] for instance, addressing we do not know what innocent souls, in a typically inconclusive work which was supposed to treat racial psychology, in his words, 'scientifically'.

We concede that, despite the ideological deformations that proceed from their premises, some results of genetic and biological research can be useful, but always, as we have said, with the proper reservations, must always be checked by super-scientific principles which will constitute the final court of appeal. An example is the Mendelian laws and their development into the so-called 'higher Mendelism'.[85] They are true and accepted, or not, depending on the reference point. Pavese has very appropriately distinguished race as 'fact' — that is, a spontaneous naturalistic effect produced by a process that is over and

---

84   Mario Canella was a Lamarckian professor of biology and zoology who worked for the Fascist Party's Racial Office from 1940. While he regarded race to be characterised by several different factors, he considered psychology to be the most important one.—Ed.

85   Gregor Johann Mendel (1822–1884) was a Czech-German scientist, and is often called 'the father of modern genetics'. Mendel's Laws of Inheritance, based on his study of plants across several generations, attempted to define how specific characteristics are transmitted from parents to their offspring.—Ed.

done with — from race as 'becoming'. For the first aspect of race, the laws are roughly exact. For the second, instead, there are no longer precise laws. Those who fail to acknowledge this distinction end up turning Mendelism into a kind of fate, which can be used, for instance, as an accessory tool in the anti-Jewish campaign, by demonstrating the inadequacy of all legislation that does not take the element of heredity into account. At the same time, however, we shall find ourselves paralysed before the essential tasks of a selective and active racism. In fact, there would be very little to do, if these laws are supposed to control race as 'becoming' (that is, what counts the most politically), if what is present in a people because of crossbreeding that took place centuries ago constitutes a fatal heritage, and if the 'dominant' and 'recessive' characteristics are supposed to remain such *ad infinitum* in everyone's body and mind. This is not the place, however, to go into technical details. It is essentially the central thesis that matters. Racists who defend the exclusive claims of the scientistic point of view, and who can coherently boast only of the gorilla and the pithecanthropus as their glorious ancestors, should be able to persuade themselves that we in Italy do not find ourselves in a Soviet regime, nor in the times of the Jacobin Enlightenment, which would mean that the adjective 'spiritual', when added to the noun 'racism', would signify shame and disrepute. We naturally prefer to define our terms, by saying that spirit, for us, does not mean either philosophical deviation or 'theosophy', or a mystical, devotional evasion, but simply what well-born people always understood by race in better times: that is, rectitude, internal integrity, character, dignity, manliness, and an immediate and direct sensitivity for all values, virtues that stand at the foundation of all human greatness and that tower over, and so dominate, the level of all contingent and material reality.

The view of race as a 'scientistic' construction and a mannequin from an anthropological museum we leave to those parts of a pseudo-intellectual middle class who are still dominated by the idols of the positivism of the nineteenth century. This is assuredly the last thing that can propitiate the awakening of that force and dignity which, in terms of racism, could only be attained in a heroic and spiritual vision of the world such as Fascism's.

Postscript. In response to the reply that was published in his magazine (*Civiltà Fascista*, June 1942), we would like to permit ourselves to draw the attention of our illustrious colleague, Pellizzi,[86] to the complex 'style' of our polemical encounter. We began by noting the appropriateness of a Race Office of the Fascist Party,[87] and in that connection, rather than propose personal discoveries, we talked about what was created in Germany at the point when people wanted to act seriously. *Critica Fascista* replied by reproving us for forgetting several initiatives undertaken by the Fascist Party and the Institute of Fascist Culture in the area of racism. We responded by taking notice of these initiatives, but asking whether, with all this, we have got any closer at all to the level of organisation and coherence to which we referred positively in, for instance, the German model. We then mentioned the principal defect, that is, of letting everyone express his opinion and the use of 'unofficial' elements which are called up to help only at the moment of harvest. Well, what could *Civiltà Fascista*[88] reply? Only this: it asked us what political and scientific authority we have for speaking about these problems. The affair is really edifying, as 'style'. Let us put on one side 'scientific' authority, because if it is a question of that science of which we have spoken in this article, we plan to have little to do with it. Even less, then, if by science the fantasies of a certain 'Idealism'

---

86   Camillo Pellizzi (1896–1979) was a professor who frequently did work on Fascist policies, and who was acquainted with Ezra Pound. In 1940 he was appointed the President of the National Institute of Fascist Culture. After the war, he was the first professor of sociology in Italy.—Ed.

87   The Race Office was subsidiary to the Ministry of Popular Culture.—Ed.

88   *Civiltà Fascista* was the journal of the National Institute of Fascist Culture, published between 1934 and 1943.—Ed.

are understood, with which we have settled our accounts in works we wrote when young.[89]

As for 'political' authority, obviously there has been a mistake. We will allow our colleague Pellizzi to decide — to deal with an extreme case — if a responsible Fascist leader will refuse to hear what will be proposed by a knowledgeable person who can think straight when dealing with coherence and organisation, in a matter of statistics or economics, for example, or whether he will instead pay more attention to a someone who is a long-time card-carrying Fascist, but who has little or no experience or vocation in these matters. One last point. *Civiltà Fascista* says that it is precisely the system of 'intellectual democracy' that is supposed to give it the way to read our writings 'with interest and curiosity'. This assertion is rash, and someone could say that it is very close to one of those 'indirect shots' to which people customarily resort when they do not know what to say in response. (It is enough to glance at the preceding number of *Vita Italiana*, pp. 155–160, where the case is found of a 'professor' [and so a person familiar with 'academic science'], wounded in the war and a member of the Fascist squads [and so familiar with the Fascist Party], who has been assigned the task of defending a Jewish philosopher.)

In any case we say loud and clear that we would be happily disposed to painfully deprive the colleagues of *Civiltà Fascista* of the pleasure of reading our writings with 'interest and curiosity', at the point when one is finally acting with authority in the area in question, according to a style of spiritual bullying (*squadrismo*), silencing newcomers, dilettantes, and compromisers. In this way, one might begin to seriously give a sense of what 'race' really is, as against the middle class, bureaucracy, and 'intellectuals'.

---

89 During the 1920s, before turning to spiritual and traditionalist matters, Evola penned a number of works on the subject of Idealist philosophy. None have been translated as of yet, but some excerpts have been made available at the *Gornahoor* Website (www.gornahoor.net).—Ed.

ARTICLES ON
NATIONAL SOCIALISM

1933—1971

Critical Observations on
National Socialist 'Racism'

(NOVEMBER 1933)

The speech recently delivered by Adolf Hitler at the cultural conference of the National Socialist Party at Nuremberg, which was reproduced by the German press with the title, 'Profession of Heroic Faith', deserves attention in our opinion for the elements it offers for understanding the famous doctrine of race that plays such an important part in the ideology of the revolution of the swastika, as is known. In fact we are dealing with official expressions of the head of this movement, which are bound to express what aspects of this doctrine National Socialism has adopted in the most official and unambiguous way. We shall here describe the principal concepts explained by Chancellor Hitler, adding to them a brief comment.

The first point, which was emphasised as a general premise, is a curious mixture of *naturalism* and *faith in providence*. It is curious, because a truly theological fatalism is placed at the foundation of a heroic vision, which directly recalls the Protestant doctrine of absolute predestination. 'Providence', says Hitler in so many words, 'has willed that men are not equal. It has determined a plurality of races and for each one has fixed special gifts and characteristics, which cannot be changed without incurring degeneration and decadence.' This is a double predestination, *biological* and *psychic* at the same time. The

111

worldviews of the various races corresponds to their intimate biological and morphological laws by which they are constrained, and which can sometimes be obvious and sometimes hidden, but which does not change essentially in the course of centuries. From this proceeds a cultural and spiritual pluralism, which in its time entered in open conflict with the universalistic views of, and was intoned catholically by, the party of the centre. Every race has its own truths and worldviews.

Hitler explicitly denies that it is possible to speak in absolute terms of a given worldview being right or wrong. A worldview can be called right or wrong only in relation to a definite race, its goals and its will to existence and power. A truth, he says, which 'is more natural to one stock, because it is innate in it and suitable for the manifestation of its life, can signify not only a serious danger but absolutely the end, in different situations, for another people who are formed differently'. Universalism and internationalism are synonyms for uncertainty, the decadence of instinct, and the loss of contact with the deepest forces of one's own people. If we may define as universal the vision in which all ethnic differences enter into a naturalistic and temporal plane, beyond which there exists a unique truth and a super-political Christian society, in which there is neither Aryan or Semite, neither European nor Asian, and so on — then it is certainly not possible to define the doctrine expounded by Hitler as 'orthodox', once we grant, of course, that it has been thought through and developed without intellectual compromises.

Some critical considerations are in order, however. Above all we are tempted to ask: if every truth is linked to a race and is true only for it alone, whether the very truth according to which this pluralism is believed in should be acknowledged as true only for one race, being prescribed by its particular characteristics, or whether it is a truth for all races universally and super-racially. It is the embarrassing and contradictory situation to which every form of relativism in general is condemned. In the act of proclaiming itself true, relativism comes to assume, *mutatis mutandis*,[90] precisely the characters of absolutism and universalism. But let us leave to one side this objection, which is of a general and speculative nature. One positive aspect must certainly be acknowledged in Hitler's position: his reaction against rationalist, Enlightenment, and democratic myths of European decadence. The doctrine of race is a positive value, insofar as it signifies the primacy of quality over quantity, of the differentiated over the formless, of the organic over the mechanical, and especially insofar as it proposes the ideal of a profound and living unity between spirit and life, thought and race, culture and instinct. Nevertheless, a similar ideal — concerning content — still remains undefined. Secondly, the ideal is something that, to be valid, needs to be liberated from both its fatalistic background and the naturalistic element.

About the first point, accepting the task of a creative synthesis between the innate idea of a race and the material conditions that are imposed on it, all the way to a 'crystal-clear conformity to the goal' — *kristallklar effüllten Zweckmässigkeit* — is not the same thing as resolving the fundamental problem: what content, case by case, must be active in this synthesis? How to recognise what is the task of one race, and therefore 'true', and not of another race? Here Hitler seems to be inclined towards a solution that is pragmatic — that is, practical and empiricist — when he says that it is difficult to rule on the correctness of a particular vision, that is, its right to be valid for a particular race, except on the basis of the consequences and effects that result from it among the men who have assumed it. This view becomes problematic, and we might almost say, 'experimental'. The famous predestination on the part of 'providence' becomes a myth that serves at best as a

90   Latin: 'by the right of one's office.'—Ed.

'force-idea'; that is, it reinforces suggestively a given vocation or per-
suasion. Nothing is objectively said about a criterion that can justify *a
priori* and link precisely a given mission or truth to a given race. It is
a little curious that Hitler conceives heroism itself as a mere 'datum'.
Just as cats or elephants give birth to offspring of their own species and
each species has its own characteristics, so also heroes or non-heroes
would beget heroic or non-heroic offspring. The heroic man thinks
and acts heroically by nature and racial characteristics, or rather by
predestination, not by a free inner action. Hitler also said that every
action that does not conform to the innate ethnic and spiritual characteristic is only a way of decadence. So, for instance, in every race
predestined to be non-heroic, every effort to assume heroic truth and
raise oneself heroically would be a way of decadence.

There is an additional issue. A fundamental point is the difference
of 'Nordic and Aryan' man from the characteristics of the man of other
races. This point is *not* resolved by Hitler — at least in the context of the
speech we are now examining — insofar as he simply describes, as being characteristic of 'Nordic and Aryan man', the traits of having always
produced 'a determining synthesis among the tasks set before him, his
goal, and the given material', both in antiquity and in modern times,
by means of his free creative spirit. In fact this difference is reduced to
the difference between people who know how to organically realise
their nature in their own lifestyle and people who do not. But are there
not, perhaps, different lifestyles? 'Classically' realising one's own mode
of being is an ideal that can be achieved on the basis of characteristics
that may be Hellenic or Hebraic, Japanese or German. The concept
remains undefined and the characteristic traits of the famous 'Nordic
and Aryan' element remain unclear. More positively, Hitler hints at an
opposition due to an innate inclination in certain races to transcend
the naturalistic element, the primitive substratum of existence, in order to transform the general traits of one's own life. This is, however,

only a hint. He barely touches on everything that was inspired by the 'supernatural' and 'twice-born' (*dvija*) character belonging to the *arya* in opposition to the *asurya* in the ancient traditions, the 'dark' man who is dominated by the 'demonic' element of nature.

Moreover, a further question is posed from the critical viewpoint. Granted that Hitler is not thinking of raising up seers capable of directly learning the foreordained plans of divine providence to order the different tasks and destinies of the races; granted that, as we have seen, there is no criterion to *a priori* determine the spiritual element that a given race will have to achieve demiurgically — the danger exists of ending in pure naturalism, and so in materialism. We mean that we can always suspect that, instead of a creative and heroic adherence of the race to the idea, there would be a simple subordination of the idea to what is given as race. In other words, the simple constitution of a given race, what is found to exist naturalistically or even (in the empirical sense) historically, and whatever it acquires by a brute will to existence and power, could become the only criteria by which that given race will pragmatically decide on the truth, validity, and congeniality of elements belonging to a higher plane, whether metabiological, spiritual, or cultural.

We want to emphasise the importance of this consideration, which highlights the reef on which racism could end up. Especially in today's world, with the breaking out of forces of an inferior and collective character on every side, it is essential to consider this dilemma: *either spirit that gives form to race* (particularly a nation) *or race* (nation) *that gives form to spirit.* Still more briefly: *either determination from above or determination from below.* People who believe that there is something fallacious and quibbling in this juxtaposition are not aware of one of the greatest problems on the contemporary political horizon.

As we have already shown on other occasions in this journal, there exist two distinct types of racism and nationalism: one is *spiritual,* the other *materialist* and subversive. The fact that both constitute a contrast to democratic and internationalist levelling and liberalist disintegration should not lead us to confuse them in the least. In one case, we have the emergence of a pre-personal (and therefore promiscuous) substratum of a given stock, which as 'soul of the race' acquires a mystic nimbus, claims for itself a sovereign right, and does not acknowledge any value in spirit, intellectualism, and culture except insofar as they transform themselves into tools in the service of a temporal and political entity. In this case, race and nation really establish a disintegrating pluralism and set themselves up in a multiplicity of antagonistic concepts, which by their nature cannot admit any higher and unitary reference point. This is when racism acquires a sense that is ethnically and collectivistically conditioned, which we have said to be in inevitable contrast with any universalist vision, such as, for instance, Catholicism's.

But things are very different when nation and race are presented truly and not rhetorically as spiritual and transcendent concepts, when what stands at the centre is no longer blood nor collective soul nor a tradition in the vulgar empirical sense, nor the brute will to existence and power of a group. No! It is precisely an *idea*, almost like a determining force from above. This is not the place — and anyhow we have written about this extensively in books — but we can at least mention that this character has been found in every higher type of civilisation and traditional state in antiquity, and *especially among the Aryan peoples*. In this case, racism's correctness is limited to this point: recognising that the formative action of forces that are higher than nature upon nature itself — that is, on the element that is naturalistic and biologically conditioned — must be so deep as to be translated into a definite heredity and definite 'form' or 'style' of life, which is common to a given group. It remains equally clear, however, that this heredity, form, or style is not explained in itself, does not have its own principle in itself, and is not a mere 'datum', as might be true of the characteristics of an animal species. Rather they are appearances and almost signs and consecrations of a conquest and a higher force.

Hitler wrote, 'Greeks and Romans found themselves so close to Germans because they had their roots in a single fundamental race, which is why the immortal creations of the ancient peoples exercise an attraction on their descendants who are racially related to them.' It seems to us, on the other hand, that this very question should lead to something more than mere racism. In particular, Romans and Germans agreed with one another and understood one another — and created the strongest type of civilisation that Europe has ever known — in a period, the imperial Middle Ages, that was dominated not by racist particularism, but *by a universal idea*. The Middle Ages shows us one of the most distinct examples of a super-political and super-national unity, which acted formatively from above and according to a single principle that, far from being smashed by ethnic egoisms and nationalistic prevarications, ended up being applied to different races in different forms, but also such as to create, through an intimate affinity of spirit, a *corpus*, a grandiose and marvelous *ordinatio ad unum*,[91] in which the individual does not end up frustrated but spiritually integrated.

As much as we have studied not only Hitler's writings, but also the writings of the chief National Socialist ideologues, it is still not clear to us if, in the last instance, the deep soul of the revolutionary current of the swastika is oriented toward one or the other of the two directions we discussed above. *The fundamental problem of the Europe of the future seems to us to be the following: overcoming the internationalist collapse and being reintegrated into values of quality, race, and difference; in such a way, however, so as not to end up in the pluralism of*

---

91   Latin: 'orientation towards the One', meaning God. This concept, first outlined by Saint Augustine, was one of the underlying principles of Christian and political thought during the Middle Ages.—Ed.

closed unities and of ideas that have passed into the service of matter and empirical politics, but instead in a way that leaves open the possibility of the formation of a higher, ecumenical reality that is suited to unite the nations in spirit, in a manly way, without confusing them in body.

The future will tell us in what direction the German restoration will end up orienting itself. For now it is clear that, insofar as Fascism has indissolubly joined to the idea of nation and stock a higher universal idea — the idea of Rome — it has already decisively placed the symbol that alone can have a positive value in the range of the problem we have discussed.

Is Nazism on the Way to Moscow?

(MARCH 1935)

The events of 30 June[92] in Germany have, as a whole, the following significance: a) the elimination of 'inconvenient' elements of a varied nature; b) the elimination of a movement of the extreme Left with a connection to Roehm (assault teams, the so-called 'second wave', which were already denounced by von Papen);[93] c) the elimination of an extreme Right, which was aiming to tactically utilise the Leftist elements in order to undermine National Socialism and then affirm themselves (von Schleicher).[94]

From 30 June 1934 until today, Nazism still finds itself in an oscillation that seems to be slowly settling toward the Right, even if in a moderate sense. The movement's centre seems, that is, to have moved

---

92 30 June 1934 marked the beginning of the Night of the Long Knives, a period which lasted until 2, when the Nazis arrested and executed many of their political opponents, allegedly to prevent a coup by the Stormtroopers (SA). The victims were not all part of the SA, however, and the Nazis used the opportunity to eliminate many of their rivals in the conservative establishment as well.—Ed.

93 Franz von Papen (1879–1969) had served as an officer in the war, then joined the Centre Party. In 1932, he was appointed by Hindenburg to be Chancellor of Germany, although he was forced to resign after only a few months. In January 1933 he urged Hindenburg to appoint Hitler, believing that he could be controlled and the Nazis used as a tool by the conservatives. After being marginalised by them, he resigned following the Night of the Long Knives.—Ed.

94 Kurt von Schleicher (1882–1934) was a Reichswehr general who sought to make the military the most powerful player in German politics again, and heavily involved in the machinations that eventually brought Hitler to power, believing that Hitler could be used as a pawn by the more mainstream conservatives. He served as Minister of Defence in von Papen's government. When von Papen resigned as Chancellor in December 1932, von Schleicher succeeded him, but his brief administration was beset by too many problems and he was dismissed after less than two months, bringing Hitler to power. He was killed during the Night of the Long Knives.—Ed.

away from the influence of the assault teams in order to move under the influence of the Reichswehr.[95] It is possible, however, that this development will not have a completely regular course (rumours of appointing Goering to replace von Papen) and that a reaction of the strictly 'revolutionary' elements will take place at a certain moment, among whom there are people who have talked about Hitler's 'betrayal'. It could therefore be useful to know what these elements want, what their ideology is, and according to what ideals they want to restore Germany by means of National Socialism.

To learn the answers to these questions we have the help of a book that was published on the eve of the Nazi revolution, and could therefore enjoy complete freedom of expression, defining clearly and courageously concepts that today, naturally, do not appear openly as such, but all the same do not cease to be valued by the elements of Nazism we have just mentioned. We are alluding to Carl Dryssen, *The Message of the East: Fascism, National Socialism, and Prussianism*,[96] which has a striking cover featuring a photomontage in which the figures of Mussolini, Hitler, and Cardinal Gasparri[97] mingle against a red background, along with assault divisions on parade with unfurled flags under the Brandenburg Gate.

The author develops his thoughts on the level of pure economic politics, but fails even within these rather narrow horizons. Two worlds in opposition are supposed to exist, more or less separated by the Rhine, which he calls 'East' and 'West'. For Dryssen the 'West' means the world of liberalism, democracy, internationalism, and then, in a word, capitalism. North America, France, and England are supposed

---

95 The Reichswehr was the name of the German military from 1919 until 1935.—Ed.

96 *Die Botschaft des Ostens : Fascismus, Nationalsozialismus und Preussentum* (Breslau: Korn, 1935).

97 Pietro Gasparri (1852–1934) was made a Cardinal in 1907. On the order of Pope Pius X, he spent 13 years compiling the first-ever codification of Roman Catholic canon law, which he completed in 1917. In 1914 he was appointed the Cardinal Secretary of State, and he signed many important concordats between the Vatican and other states, the most significant being the Lateran Accords which were signed with the Fascist government of Italy in 1929, ending the Vatican's 60-year conflict with the Italian state.—Ed.

to belong to it, with their maxims of free trade and their financial imperialism. In sum, internally the principle of individualism belongs to this system; externally the principle of imperialism. Its liberalism is hypocrisy in the service of a policy that is either hegemonic or destructive of other peoples.

For Dryssen the 'East' means, on the other hand and above all, Germany. To an industrial and capitalist type of state he opposes an essential agrarian state; to individualism the social spirit; to an imperialist and internationalist economy, an economy of consumption, with a direct relation to its own blood and soil.

According to Dryssen, the World War meant an attack of the West on the East. It marked the critical moment in which the individualist and capitalist idea jumped over the limits of its own world and became — if one can say so — explosive, attempting to overthrow and bend under its system — indifferent to blood and soil — the part of Europe that still resisted it or could resist it. Obviouslym Dryssen is here considering matters in a way that is arbitrary, or at least very one-sided. German and Nazi circles have reproached Wilhelmine Germany with certain underhanded agreements with finance capitalism and German big business, while it is known that 'territorial demands' and the principle of nationality played a preponderant role in the Allies' ideology all the way to the peace treaties.

In any event, these confusions are unimportant when compared with the ones that Dryssen commits when he goes on to examine the post-war situation, and especially the significance of Fascism.

In the ideological, social, and political chaos of the post-war period, two chief antagonistic tendencies appeared: one *Roman and reformist*, the other *German and revolutionary*, corresponding respectively to *Fascism* (as Dryssen imagines it) and *National Socialism* (as Dryssen hopes it will be, and as it exists in the minds of the Left-wing hoodlums we have mentioned.)

For Dryssen, Fascism does not possess a truly revolutionary character, in the sense that it has not led to a type of state that is really different from the 'Western' state, that is, individualist and capitalist. Harking back to the prejudices of who knows what antiquated and myopic schema from historical materialism, Dryssen claims, moreover, that ancient Rome and later the canon law formulated by the Church of Rome and its praxis would never have led beyond the 'Western' world. The Roman ideal of *pax* and *justitia*[98] is supposed to have the mere significance of a system of social equilibrium and normalisation that worked on premises that were essentially individualistic and capitalistic, and the social ideology of the Church did not follow a substantially different course. For Dryssen, Fascism has not distanced itself from this tradition. Once its original revolutionary impulse was 'tamed' (*bezähmt*) and 'rendered socialist', it did not signify a revolt against the old system, but only a correction of it. Fascism recognises both private property and private initiative, and only removes the rough patches and unbalanced swings that are found in the class struggle and unbridled liberal capitalism. Therefore it leads to an *authoritarian capitalism* sustained by state control, by which the fundamental elements of the old 'Western' system are not only acknowledged, but strengthened and removed from the salutary crisis that other countries are in the process of overthrowing. 'Revolution' is avoided. In addition, Fascism maintains the imperialist tendency, which is 'a vocation inseparable from the Roman tradition'. It is not content with its validity as a national political ideal, but, directly or indirectly, it presents itself beyond Italy's borders as an example. However, insofar as Rome succeeds in its role as saviour of Western capitalism in its death throes, it represents a new danger for the German anti-capitalist and 'socialist' tradition. For Dryssen, National Socialism is called to defend this tradition in a revolutionary manner, to continue the ancient emancipation movement

---

98   'Peace' and 'justice'.—Ed.

from Rome — *Los von Rom!*[99] — that began in the religious sphere with Luther.

In addition, for Dryssen the Lutheran revolt stands, in spirit, in the closest relationship with the German Peasants' Revolt,[100] which many German racists consider the last gasp of the Nordic will to independence. The peasants that rose against the nobility and the clergy demanded that their land pass to them in communistic form. They took their place next to the Lutheran impatience with authoritarian individualism, imperialism, urbanisation, and glorification of the world, which are all said to be 'Roman'. Basically, we are dealing with two aspects of an essentially 'socialistic' upheaval that then — all this is Dryssen's opinion — is fundamental for the Prussian tradition, which is supposed to be agrarian and anti-capitalist, because property has a social function and kings figure as 'servants of the people'. National Socialism should therefore make up its mind to be a 'social-Prussian' revolution against the West and against 'Rome'. It should stand up against the attempt to reduce Germany to a colony in service to 'Western' Europe, which was at work in the German revolution of 1918 and governed by the principles of capitalism, democracy, and internationalism, but also against the conservative and 'feudal' remnants of the German economy and against Fascist 'authoritarian capitalism'. For Dryssen, Hitler faces two alternatives: either Fascism or National Socialism; either West or East; either maintaining the capitalist system, the final product of the individualistic conception of state and economy, or a radical rejection of it and the development of a completely new economic and political structure.

---

99 'Away from Rome!' was the name of a movement which began in Austria in 1898, and encouraged German Austrians to reject Catholicism and become Lutherans as part of a Pan-Germanic nationalist vision. It was moderately successful, but disappeared after the First World War.—Ed.

100 The German Peasants' Uprising took place across the German-speaking regions of Europe in 1524 and 1525, when the peasants revolted against the authority of the aristocracy of the Holy Roman Empire, which was viewed as unjust, and was influenced by Protestantism. The aristocrats were victorious and many thousands of peasants were killed.—Ed.

Dryssen offers a vision of life that is either heroic or economic as alternatives. The German vocation is one that flees cosmopolitan culture; instinctively thinks in terms of collectivity instead of individualistically; aspires not to wealth but to power; values people and not things by cultivating a fighting spirit that is not in the service of any sort of imperialism, but rather in defence of its own soil, despising the 'cadaveric obedience' of Catholic and Jesuitical morality, and is led in a revolutionary way to every struggle without surrender for the altars of its race.

With all this, it seems to us that we have enough blunders and confusions. Like many other racist writers who, while not doing real honour to the culture of their own countries, repeat slogans in the wake of Chamberlain[101] and other dilettantes, Dryssen not only does not understand either the sense of the Roman spirit or of Fascism, but also seems to know nothing of the best tradition of the German people themselves. First of all, by declaring with all seriousness that the goal of the new Fascist system is 'power through wealth' and that the values of the ancient Roman spirit can be reduced to individualism, capitalism, and urbanism, while loyalty to soil and the asceticism of force and heroism is supposed to be a Prussian monopoly, or worse — he is talking like an irresponsible person, if not an ignoramus. Who does not know that the unity of sword and plow, the double face of Mars, the god of war and agriculture, the sacral connection to their own property among patricians, and so on, were characteristics of what can be understood as the pure and original Roman spirit, and not the decadence that was created in Rome by foreign elements? If Dryssen's horizons were not so narrow and his factious exclusivism did not amount to genuine mental obtuseness, we would be glad to acknowledge — because it is true — that we are here facing a general

---

101 Houston Stewart Chamberlain (1855–1927) was an English philosopher whose ideas about the supremacy of the Germanic peoples, as outlined in his most fundamental book, *The Foundations of the Nineteenth Century*, became highly influential upon the German racialist movement.—Ed.

Indo-European patrimony, which therefore is not a distinctive trait of either his people or ours. But this would amount to once again showing the one-sidedness of his contrasts in order to make it clear how much of what he denies in his assertions exists, and vice versa.

Dryssen shows no less blindness in relation to Fascism. The entire warrior education that Fascism seeks to give the new generations by choosing a highly significant motto, 'Life is warfare and warfare is life', the Fascist struggle against urbanism, its precise and concrete initiatives for returning to the land and agrarianism, the new dispositions in the area of law aimed at changing — just as Dryssen wants it — the motto 'property is theft' into 'property is a duty', and so on, where does Dryssen put them? Is Fascism a system of force in the service of capitalism and a purely economic ideal of life? In no way! Fascism's system of authority turns the materialist dependence of politics on economics on its head. It therefore reaffirms the subordination of economics to politics because it does not fall into the error either of socialism or liberalism, but places ahead of its economic reality, which is differentiated and free but disciplined, the higher ideal of 'nation' and then 'empire' as a reference point that is super-economic, super-individual, and spiritual. Fascism respects private property, but not in homage to 'Western' truth, but because it is among the essential material conditions for the dignity and autonomy of the person.

Dryssen makes two other serious mistakes, first, by confusing *personality* and *individuality*; then by confusing *internationalism* and *universality*. These are errors that we have had occasion to denounce in this journal, but they persist tenaciously in the dominant Nazi ideologies.

Concerning the first point, we shall repeat that it is possible to combat liberalism and individualism without saying a word against the higher ideal of *personality*. On the contrary, combating them is the premise for really understanding this ideal. Socialism and individualism are basically two integral aspects of a single material-ist, anti-qualitative, and levelling decadence that have arisen in recent times. The ideal of free, differentiated, and virile personalities as elements to create an organic and hierarchical political reality where each person has his own function and his own dignity is superior to both socialism and liberalism. Moreover this ideal is especially and generically Indo-European, then Classical, Classical Roman, and, finally, Roman and Germanic (medieval). So Dryssen can become as angry as he wants with the liberalistic, democratic, and individualistic 'West'. Neither the Roman spirit nor Fascism has anything in common with this 'West'. In reality, we are dealing here with a relatively recent phenomenon that emerged from the ferment of the decomposition of our common culture, which can only illegitimately be called the West. To the socialism that, as the 'solidarity of the working class', expresses only a sentiment of inferiority cemented by envy for those who own property, Dryssen opposes a socialism not of 'having' but of 'being', not of hate but of dignity, based on an 'aristocratic corporatism' in the higher sense, on disdain for wealth, on returning to the soil and the sentiment that every urbanistic opulence is a poison. In this he is deceiving himself that he has delineated a 'Prussian' tradition. On the contrary, these are values that our tradition already possesses and that Fascism has reclaimed to a certain degree, and which, finally, were a common patrimony in medieval culture. *Therefore, the fact is that what Dryssen calls the 'West' is only a recent decadence of the true, traditional West, and while he tries to locate us in this decadence, making of every blade of grass a bundle in the name of anti-Rome, the truth is that his own reference points are to be labelled 'Western' in his sense of perversion and contemporary decadence.*

In fact, the soul of Dryssen's 'Prussian' anti-Roman spirit — aside from 'anti-capitalism', which plays the part of an *idée fixe* with him — is *Luther*. In other words, the man who was the first to foment that individualistic and anti-hierarchical revolt that, little by little, was fated to move into the political field, and to the revolt of the German princes against the universal and 'Roman' principle of the Empire, and from there to the revolt of the democratically conceived nations, which was fated to lead straight to our contemporary individualistic disintegration. Instead of commending that which, could have attained to the large-scale initiative in his own nobler German tradition, as in, for instance, the Ghibelline[102] idea, Dryssen completely repudiates this tradition. In the name of Luther, 'Prussian socialism',[103] anti-capitalism, and the 'message of the East' he is going to end up — where? — in the arms of *Lenin*. No more and no less.

Dryssen wonders whether, at the end of the day, a true spiritual frontier really exists between the Elbe and the Urals, and without hesitation he points to Bolshevik Russia as the only great power that has decisively set itself up today against the 'West', Rome, and capitalism. He says that for a German who has made up his mind to rid himself of everything that is foreign and plans to change his essence from 'Western', the fear of turning into a Bolshevik is a childish fear. When its real cause is understood, Nazism's 'social' revolution must lead as far from capitalism and individualism as Bolshevism, since Nazism and Bolshevism have the ideal of a socialised state, agrarian and armed, in common, where in a collectivism of its native soil the ancient German

---

102 Ghibelline is a thirteenth century term which was originally coined to name the supporters of the imperial power of the Hohenstaufen throne against Papal authority. They were in conflict with the Guelphs, who favoured the rule of the Pope. Evola saw this conflict as highlighting the distinction between priestly and royal authority in the state, since he believed the Ghibelline view to be the only valid one from a traditional perspective. He discusses this at length in *Revolt Against the Modern World* and *The Mystery of the Grail.*—Ed.

103 The term Prussian socialism was first coined by Oswald Spengler in an essay of the same name. He held that the organisation of the modern Prussian state had always been in accordance with socialist principles, albeit of a communitarian and hierarchical type.—Ed.

system of the *Almende*[104] would meet that of the ancient Slavic *mir*,[105] in new forms.

There is more. As the final apotheosis of the message of the 'East', the hierophant Dryssen predicts that Luther and Lenin are embracing like brothers. Soviet atheism — Dryssen affirms with complete tranquillity — is an empty bogeyman, meant to lead us by the nose. In reality, it represents the spirit of the Reformation: it is a rebellion against official religiosity, which is superficial, Romanised, secularised, and authoritarian, bound by earthy riches. It is precisely from this kind of revolt that a new piety can develop, one that is true, inner, free, and social, as it was in the aspiration of Luther, prophet of the German people liberated from the Roman yoke.

With this, we see Dryssen make a hard crash-landing after his timid gestures of flying, represented by his conception of an 'aristocratic socialism' (which, however, the oldest form of our Roman Senate can claim for its own) and by references to the asceticism of force and the heroic Prussian style. Once he has said 'no' to the ideal of a Roman *universality*, and in his infantile fear of a presumed 'Fascist imperialism' (almost as though Mussolini had not spoken of this empire 'that has no need to conquer even a square kilometre of territory to realise itself' — and as if, on the other hand, *Deutschland über alles, über alles in der Welt* were the anthem of…German agrarian anti-imperialism), he falls into the arms of the Bolshevik anthem, the 'Internationale'.[106] He really seems not to know that the concepts of fatherland and nation have no place in the Soviet system, and still less the concept of a tradition where the land can count for anything more than material and

---

104 *Almende* was the system of property ownership by village communities in medieval Germany, by which land was also distributed to the peasants for farming.—Ed.

105 In medieval Russia, a *mir* was a self-governing peasant community which oversaw the equitable redistribution of land among its members.—Ed.

106 The 'Internationale', which calls for socialist principles to be adopted universally, was first composed by French socialists in the late nineteenth century, and was adopted as the anthem of the early Soviet Union. In 1944 it was replaced by the more nationalistic 'Hymn of the Soviet Union'.—Ed.

clods of clay, and that the Communist abolition of private property is only one episode in a much vaster initiative aiming at the abolition of the very concept of personality, of every autonomous faculty, and of every interest, however detached from that of collective man, omnipotent and materialistic, who has risen up to 'redeem' humanity in a faceless, proletarianised mass.

With this, I believe we have said enough. It would be all too easy to demolish an ideology like his point by point. The value we find in this ideology is not logical, but that of a *symptom*. History shows us that the ideas that have had the greatest effect are not the most well-founded ones, but those that could accumulate the suggestive power of a force-idea in themselves, making it a centre of crystallisation, so to speak, for the confused tendencies of an environment. Next to Dryssen, we could cite other Nazi authors, whose affirmations reveal a similar spirit. For instance, Darré,[107] who is a Nazi minister, is the author of a book entitled *Das Bauerntum als Lebensquell der nordischen Rasse*,[108] a book that has created a furore in Germany and possesses an almost official character. In it, Darré mounts the old hobbyhorses of 'agrarian socialism': the old, passionate denunciations of imperialism, which he claims was never a Nordic principle, and the tired protests against the concept of private property and capitalism. Moreover, Darré did not hesitate to profess the same repudiation of German aristocratic traditions that we have already found in Dryssen in a well-known speech, and goes further by proclaiming not only the Hohenzollerns[109] and the

---

107 Richard Walther Darré (1895-1953) was the Minister of Food and Agriculture in the Third Reich from 1933 until 1942, and was also one of the top leaders of the SS. He was one of the primary proponents of the 'blood and soil' concept. Darré pioneered developments in organic farming and conservation.—Ed.

108 *The Agrarian Class as the Source of Life of the Nordic Race* (Munich: J F Lehmanns, 1929). No English version exists.—Ed.

109 The House of Hohenzollern is a noble family which contributed many monarchs to Germany, Prussia, and Rumania over the course of nearly a thousand years.—Ed.

Habsburgs,[110] but even the Hohenstaufens[111] as traitors to the German race.

After all, readers have already found a report on the new, vain ambitions for an anti-Roman and racist law in these pages, a 'social law based on blood'. They may be aware that people no longer speak of Charlemagne in Germany, but instead refer to him as Charles the Frank, who, because he took up the principle of Roman universality, is being blamed for Germany's worst ills.[112] Readers know that Rosenberg actually said that National Socialism's 'Third Reich' does not have its precedents in the tradition of the old Sacrum Imperium,[113] but rather in the tradition of all the rebels against the Roman and imperial principle, especially Widukind, the Saxon chief and proud enemy of Charlemagne, who was overwhelmed in the tenth century[114] but is now destined to rise victorious in the figure of Adolf Hitler. We could go on for some time with quotations of this type. This is an anti-aristocracy, socialism, an illusory 'Nordic' tradition as pretext for an anti-tradition, an ugly anti-Roman affair that ends in philo-Bolshevism.

All this taken together tells us about the nature of one of the possibilities that Nazism has presented, a negative one, which seems to be gradually losing influence today. It cannot, however, be considered completely bypassed, and at a certain point a decisive stance toward it will have to be taken in the field of practical politics. Given the part that Germany, directly or indirectly, plays in central Europe, since the face that Germany will ultimately present cannot be a matter of indifference

---

110 The Habsburgs were the ruling family of the Austro-Hungarian Empire (previously the Austrian Empire), which was a loose confederation of Central European states centred in Vienna.—Ed.

111 The Hohenstaufens were a German noble family which produced several of the Emperors of the Holy Roman Empire, including Frederick the Great. They ruled over regions of Germany and Sicily.—Ed.

112 Charlemagne attempted to convert the Saxons to Christianity, causing them to rebel against him. In October 782, during this war, Charlemagne had 4,500 Saxons massacred in retaliation for casualties they had inflicted upon him. As a consequence, some of the Nazi leadership, especially Himmler and Rosenberg, considered Charlemagne to be an enemy of the Germans.—Ed.

113 The Latin form of the Holy Roman Empire.—Ed.

114 He actually lived in the eighth century.—Ed.

toward the overall development of the culture of our continent, we can only hope that overcoming similar tendencies may be accomplished rapidly and decisively. In Italy we have our own precise way, which has nothing in common with either the Freemasonic, democratic, and liberal West, or with the Bolshevising and socialistic 'East'. It is not up to us, but to Germany herself and the role she could still play in the future, to formulate the hope that her best forces can lead her beyond this paralysing opposition and onto the road to a real reconstruction.

On the Differences between the Fascist and Nazi Conception of the State

(April 1941)

As many people know, one point where the Fascist conception differs from the National Socialist one concerns the idea of the state in its relation to the idea of the nation. The goal of these notes is to characterise this difference, to see to what point it is real and finally to examine and clarify the viewpoint from which a real or possible difference can be overcome. Naturally, this is a question of a simple contribution to a complicated problem, which deserves a fuller treatment.

Fascism affirms the 'moral personality' of the state and the priority of the state before the nation. We can refer to well-known expressions of the Duce himself: 'Fascism reaffirms the State as the only true expression of the individual'; 'for the Fascist, all is comprised in the State and spiritual or human exists — much less has any value — outside the State'; 'the nation does not beget the State, according to the decrepit naturalistic concept which was used as a basis for the publicists of the national states in the Nineteenth century. On the contrary, the nation is created by the State, which gives the people, conscious of their own moral unity, the will, and thereby an effective existence'; 'The Fascist state organises the nation'.[115]

---

115 'The Doctrine of Fascism', pp. 29–30, 43.—Ed.

About the 'people' so dear to democratic ideology, Mussolini speaks as of a 'mysterious entity', in the sense of a myth, of something flimsy and unreliable. This is why he says that 'regimes can be called democratic which, from time to time, give the people the illusion of being sovereign, whereas the real and effective sovereignty exists in other, and very often secret and irresponsible forces'.[116] Finally, Mussolini reaffirms the spirituality of the state: 'The State as conceived and enacted by Fascism is a spiritual and moral fact since it gives concrete form to the political, juridical and economical organization of the country. Furthermore this organization as it rises and develops, is a manifestation of the spirit'.[117] 'The State, inasmuch as it transcends the short limits of individual lives, represents the immanent conscience of the nation'.[118] 'The Fascist State, the highest and the most powerful form of personality is a force, but a spiritual one. It reassumes all the forms of the moral and intellectual life of man'.[119] In this sense, Mussolini speaks of the state as of a form of the nation's 'entelechy'. It is the 'soul of the soul'. 'It is inner form and norm'.

We have intentionally taken these expressions from Mussolini's 'Doctrine of Fascism'.[120] It is therefore a question of fundamental official views, not of phrases taken from speeches delivered on one occasion or another.

Passing now to the National Socialist conception, we shall refer equally directly to the words of Hitler that are contained in *Mein Kampf*. It is necessary, however, to make an etymological preface concerning

---

116 Ibid., p. 37.—Ed.

117 Ibid., p. 41.—Ed.

118 Ibid., p. 42.—Ed.

119 Ibid., p. 31.—Ed.

120 In 1932 an article, 'The Doctrine of Fascism', was published under Mussolini's name. This was an official article which was composed by the philosopher Giovanni Gentile and approved by Mussolini and published in the *Enciclopedia Italiana* 14, and which was included in *Mussolini's Opera Omnia*, volume 34. It has been regarded as the most definitive statement of Italian Fascist doctrine. The full text is available at www.gutenberg.org/files/14058/14058-h/14058-h.htm#THE_DOCTRINE_OF_FASCISM.—Ed.

the meaning of the German word *Volk*, a word that has various con-
notations. It can mean nation, people, stock, and even race. 'People as
race' would perhaps be the most suitable translation. In contrast with
the Fascist conception, the National Socialist one is characterised by
an emphasis given to the *Volk*, the people, and the race, as opposed to
the state. Hitler writes, '[T]he State is not an end in itself but the means
to an end. It is the preliminary condition under which alone a higher
form of human civilization can be developed, but it is not the source
of such a development. This is to be sought exclusively in the actual
existence of a race which is endowed with the gift of cultural creative-
ness. There may be hundreds of excellent States on this earth, and yet
if the Aryan, who is the creator and custodian of civilization, should
disappear, all culture that is on an adequate level with the spiritual
needs of the superior nations today would also disappear.'[121] 'We must
make a clear-cut distinction between the vessel and its contents. The
State is only the vessel and the race is what it contains.'[122] Hitler continues, 'The vessel can have a meaning only if it preserves and safeguards
the contents. Otherwise it is worthless. Hence the supreme purpose
of the ethnical State is to guard and preserve those racial elements
which, through their work in the cultural field, create that beauty and
dignity which are characteristic of a higher mankind.'[123] On the other
hand, a state can be described as not corresponding to its mission, and
therefore evil, when, 'in spite of the existence of a high cultural level, it
dooms to destruction the bearers of that culture by breaking up their
racial uniformity.'[124]

Here, naturally, we can notice a certain repositioning of the problem. It is less a question of the state *per se* than of the human material

---

121   Adolf Hitler, *Mein Kampf*, translated by James Murphy (London: Hutchinson, 1939), p. 211.—Ed.

122   Ibid., p. 213.—Ed.

123   Ibid., p. 213.—Ed.

124   Ibid.—Ed.

destined to play the most important part in it. In all events, the negation of the personality of the state is clear here, since it is conceived as
the simple tool of the *Volk*, the people-race. This negation is reflected
in the lack of a true authority, raised high over the nation. *Dux*[125] and
Führer are usually considered as analogous expressions. They are
analogous from the etymological viewpoint, because the Latin *ducere*,
from which *Dux* comes, corresponds to German *führen*, from which
Führer. There is, however, a difference.

Let us disregard the fact that the Fascist *Dux* is the head of the government, not the head of state, since this latter function belongs to the
monarchy, which represents the stability and continuity of the government, of the stock, and tradition. Even ignoring this fact, the *Führer*
is rather different from the *Dux* because he has the authority — literally — of a 'guide'. He is less someone who dominates and more
someone who guides or directs. He is less someone who creates than
someone who interprets and stands at the head of a 'people', assuming
this function almost through a mandate and common agreement. *Die
Weihe des Führertums ist das Volk.*[126] This phrase characterises this
state of affairs: the *Führer* draws his legitimacy and authority from the
Volk. This is why in Italy — with good reason — the word 'socialism'
always preserves a suspect and unpleasant connotation, which it does
not have in Germany, where it figures in the name of the Party, which
is called — let us not forget it — National Socialist, i.e., national and
socialist.

It is worthwhile to examine this difference between the two ideologies in the area of law. Point 19 of the Nazi Party's platform contains the
following words: 'We ask that a German common law replace Roman

---

125 Latin: 'duke'.—Ed.

126 'The people is the consecration of leadership.'—Ed.

law, the slave of a materialistic world order.'[127] In order to understand what 'Roman law' means here, we refer to the view of Helmut Nicolai.[128] For Nicolai, Rome at its origins acknowledged a law still permeated with virility and ethical responsibility, but the mixing of blood and races in an ethnic chaos took place in Rome's first period. On top of this now ruined substance, covered with Levantines, Africans, and Metics,[129] rose the Roman *imperium* like an enormous, soulless state machine. Next to it, no longer possessing any connection with blood, 'Roman law' took form. This 'Roman' law is therefore supposed to rest on a political unity that is foreign to peoples and rules them from outside. It developed on positivistic, rationalistic, and universalistic bases, with abstract formulations of laws as rigid in the letter as they were arbitrary and easy to disregard in any practical terms. 'In the Roman juridical conception' — Nicolai continues — 'law is what the arbitrarily discriminating power of the state decrees. In the racist conception, on the other hand, law is an eternal ethical greatness that stands above the powers of the state and cannot be changed by the state. In the Roman conception, right is what stands in the law — *positum*, whence "positivism". In the racist conception, law is only what conforms to an eternal juridical idea. In the first conception, what can be justified with the letter is legal; form yields place to content. The star that guides us in the first is conformity to paragraphs; in the second it is conscience.' Naturally, it is not a question of the consciousness of natural law, which is general and equal for all, but a consciousness that is differentiated and conditioned by race.

---

127 This comes from the '25 Points' that were announced as the fledgling Party's programme by Hitler on 24 February 1920. Although never officially abrogated, most of its points were forgotten after the Party took power.—Ed.

128 Helmut Nicolai (1895–1955) was a German lawyer who was a member of the Nazi Party and who was prominent in the early years of Nazi rule, especially in drafting the Nuremberg racial laws. He drew the ire of the Party in 1935, however, when he suggested that the power of the *Führer* should be limited by a council and that the Nazi Party should dissolve itself once its tasks had been completed. He was charged with treason, but, confessing to his crimes, was pardoned, but was excluded from all political or Party offices.—Ed.

129 Metics were people who resided in the city-state of Athens but who were not Athenian citizens.—Ed.

Let us therefore return to race as the source of juridical forms, and so also of whatever 'positive' element exists in the state structure. The consequence is a curious interaction between law and racism — racism as race hygiene. This is the reason for the motto: *Verteidigung der Rasse durch das Recht* — that is, defence of the race by means of the law. Already in 1926, the German Minister of Justice, Hans Frank, proclaimed as law 'everything that works for the advantage of the *Volk*, the people-race' and as 'anti-law everything that is harmful to it'. Falk Ruttke[130] goes even further. 'More than defending the race by means of law, it is a question of consolidating and reinforcing German blood with respect to the theory of race and heredity', since, by speaking this way, the active element of the measures to be taken would be much more prominent than a purely defensive one. This point is a logical consequence of removing the positive element from the idea of law. Alfred Rosenberg had already mentioned this ancient Indo-Aryan expression: 'Law and unlaw do not walk around and say: We are this. Law is what Aryan men discover to be right.'[131] He then added, 'This is an allusion to a primordial wisdom forgotten in the present day that law is a blood related scheme. It is a system of religion and art. It is linked for eternity to a certain blood with which it appears and with which it passes away.'[132] From this viewpoint, Ruttke is right when he says that it is not up to the law to defend the race, but rather from the reintegration of the race the reintegration of the law must follow. Only the man who is pure of race will be able to have the right sense of the law — naturally, not law in general, but the law that is adapted to the people to which he belongs.

---

130   Falk Ruttke (1894–1955) was a German jurist who helped to draft the Nazi eugenics laws.—Ed.

131   Alfred Rosenberg, *The Myth of the Twentieth Century* (Torrance, California: Noontide Press, 1982), p. 126.—Ed.

132   Ibid.—Ed.

In these terms, there would seem to be a real difference concerning the views of Fascism and National Socialism on the state and law. Is it a question of an antithesis, or of differences that allow the possibility of a reciprocal integration and deepening of both viewpoints?

We have already mentioned the part changing perspectives play in such differences. The Nazi conception can be said to proceed from the viewpoint of a revolution still taking place, while the Fascist conception rather suggests the viewpoint of a revolution that is already consolidated, and so intent on giving life to lasting and stable forms.

We note that both viewpoints are opposed to the purely juridical conception of sovereignty. As Costamagna[133] has mentioned in this journal, a juridical conception differs from a political conception by its no longer attributing sovereignty to a man or a group of men, but to the so-called independent entity that wants to be acknowledged in the personality of the state. Basically, the juridical doctrine has been accepted because it claims to lead to an impersonal solution of the problem of power, and because it presented the advantage that the holder of power, whoever he might be, could not claim to exercise power on its own account, but rather in the interest of the society, so that its own possession of power becomes illegitimate when it loses sight of its goal. But even with this interpretation, which is of a democratic complexion and which has been added by Michoud,[134] there still remains the problem of the *form* of a given juridical system, a problem that constitutes the eternal stumbling block of the formalistic and positive conception of law. It still poses, that is, the problem that relates to law's *principium individuationis*,[135] of the 'sufficient reason' through which

---

133 Carlo Costamagna (1881–1965) was a Fascist intellectual who published the political journal, *Lo Stato* (The State), to which Evola contributed. He was also one of the signatories of the 1938 Race Manifesto of Fascism. Costamagna argued that the state should not rely on force to obtain the loyalty of its subjects, but rather should become the moral example for the people to follow.—Ed.

134 Léon Michoud (1855–1916) was a French jurist who specialised in administrative law.—Ed.

135 Latin: 'principle of individuation', by which a thing is distinguished from other things.—Ed.

law and, finally, the state itself have one given form and not another in its actual structure.

National Socialism particularly emphasises the forces that determine this form, which cannot fall from heaven (at least where it is no longer a question of traditional cultures in the higher sense), but which is created by men and races of men. From this viewpoint it is correct to say that the state and law represent something secondary in respect to the quality of the men who are their creators. Laws are good to the extent that they remain forms that adhere to the original demands and tools fitted to strengthen and confirm those forces that have awakened them to life. This, however, is also the Fascist viewpoint.

Fascism certainly does not accept as its own either the view of an impersonal 'juridical sovereignty' or that of 'Roman law' as the National Socialists interpret it, however abusively. The state whose sovereignty and primacy Fascism proclaims is not something abstract or automatic. To prove this is the fact that, apart from the supreme reference point, the source of all legitimacy that is constituted by the monarchy (which, however, is itself not impersonal and abstract, but a supremely personalised reality) — apart from this, behind the Fascist state stands the Fascist movement and party, and this state is the revolutionary state, that is, the state renewed by Fascism.

If we want to find differences, the problem would therefore have to be moved to another level. Since both National Socialism and Fascism acknowledge a *dynamis*, a deep force that establishes and animates the state and is the deep principle of its authority and sovereignty, it is a question of defining the nature attributed in both cases to this *dynamis*, or *ratio existentiae*,[136] so to speak, of the state in its concreteness. The 'myth' of National Socialism, in this respect, is the race or race-people,

---

136 Latin: 'sufficient reason'. In some philosophical doctrines, the idea of sufficient reason stipulates that everything that exists has a reason for doing so.—Ed.

as we have seen. It is a question here of understanding what is meant and not being satisfied with simple words.

Let us return to Mussolini's 'Doctrine of Fascism', and precisely to the ninth paragraph of the first part. Having already described the people as a 'mysterious entity', Mussolini repeats that 'Fascism for this reason is opposed to the democracy which identifies peoples with the greatest number of individuals and reduces them to a majority level'.[137] He affirms, on the other hand, a qualitative conception, a conception of the 'most coherent and truest form and is therefore the most moral, because it sees a people realised in the consciousness and will of the few or even of one only; an ideal which moves to its realisation in the consciousness and will of all. By "all" is meant all who derive their justification as a nation, ethnically speaking, from their nature and history, and who follow the same line of spiritual formation and development as one single will and consciousness'. Mussolini adds, 'not as a race nor as a geographically determined region, but as a progeny that is rather the outcome of a history which perpetuates itself; a multitude unified by an idea embodied in the will to have power and to exist, conscious of itself and of its personality'. He concludes, 'This higher personality is truly the nation, inasmuch as it is the State'.[138]

Does this confirm the difference between the two movements, especially and specifically with reference to race? We do not believe so. Fascism too has claimed racism, but not, however, the racism that is a myth with a zoological base. Nor should race mean for us, through an unfair interpretation, a new way for the democratic deviation or socialising ideologies to appear.

The nation and the state cannot be 'race' in the naturalistic sense, as has been affirmed not only by Mussolini but also by the most intransigent German racists, because they recognise precisely and without

---

137 'The Doctrine of Fascism', p. 30.—Ed.

138 Ibid.—Ed.

difficulty that all nations corresponding to today's states are not 'races', but mixtures of different races. Mussolini's view is as follows: there is a generic quality that can be called 'nation' or even 'nation-race', which is not purely anthropological and is found diffused in all components of a given political unity, so to speak, in different quantities and amounts. This makes it possible to think that, while in some it is latent and obstructed, in others it is more actual, more self-conscious, and more realised, until it becomes absolute and pure in an elite or a leader, and is manifested as precise consciousness and precise will to power and life. In a current with a base that is also ethnic and racial, as stock, and defined by the same line of spiritual development and formation, this elite then becomes the central and dominating thread, the element that transforms and reawakens and, concerning other parts, is the soul as an animating force that is also formative and which provides the body's self-awareness. The state's sovereignty and its priority in respect to the 'people' and the nation are symbols for this action of the elite and a chief.

Does a fundamental difference exist in these terms between the Fascist idea and the National Socialist one? The difference is not fundamental, unless we make of race, on which National Socialism insists so much, a mythic entity, like the democratic 'people' Mussolini speaks of so ironically. Even concerning Germany, what does race basically mean? We just now mentioned that German racists admit that even their own people is a mixture of races. Some will say that it is not a question of race in general, but of the Aryan race and then, actually, the Nordic race. In fact, Hitler talks about the Aryan race as the creator of cultures, and more specifically he thinks that the Nordic race — one of the six principle races contained in the German mixture — has this quality to an eminent degree. But here too it is necessary to get to the bottom of the matter. The Aryan quality is the requirement for full German citizenship, for being the *Volksgenosse* or 'stock companion', who enjoys all civil and political rights as opposed to being a simple member of the German state, a *Staatsangehöriger*.[139] This 'Aryan' quality is defined in purely negative terms. To possess it, it is enough to be not entirely Hebrew, or to be from the races of colour, nor to have the blood of these races in one's own ancestors as far as the third generation back. At best, a clause has been added which insists on one not having any hereditary illnesses that would provoke sterilisation, or to show those congenital inclinations that are defined in Germany as the so-called 'asocial' qualities. But all these traits are too insignificant for purity of race. Is this enough only because there is direct evidence of what is true law, beyond every 'positive' law and because it is possible to contribute to the highest spiritual elevation of the state?

Should we speak, instead of Aryan in general, rather of 'Nordic'? Then we shall have to pose the problem of selection, since the German race is not composed of Nordic elements alone, as conversely Nordic elements are found in other nations that are not German. No one in Germany is so radical as to draw all the conclusions that follow from the thesis that the Nordic race is the superior one, which would mean that only members of this race could be entrusted with either the administration of law or the work of the development of the National Socialist state. Even if the supreme hierarchies of this state are composed of 'Aryan' elements, they are certainly not composed exclusively, at least so far, of purely Nordic elements.

There is another point. In a speech he delivered in 1933 in Nuremberg, Hitler correctly acknowledged that the Nordic physical form can be found without the corresponding spiritual elements, so that, in this respect, the final criterion must be given by examining the attitude of soul and spirit, of character, and of works. He is admitting discrimination within the Nordic element itself. Finally, we should recall the assertion of one of the best-known German racists and

139 'Citizen'.—Ed.

supporters of the Nordic thesis, L F Clauss,[140] who has acknowledged that racial purity should not be conceived in terms of the collectivity, that is, numerically and statistically, but rather in terms of purity of type. Even if all the individuals of a given ethnic group can be called Nordic in a general sense, only a few are truly Nordic and manifest this race in a pure and perfect form.

These statements correspond almost to the letter with Mussolini's, when he talks about an idea that 'is realised in the consciousness and will of the few', although 'an ideal which moves to its realisation in the consciousness and will of all'.[141] Some will point out that there is an explicit reference to race in National Socialism. This is true. But, as we have said just now, Hitler himself ends up acknowledging that, when all is said and done, the true and decisive criterion of race must be sought in the spiritual element. This is why an in-depth examination 'race' as found in Nazi political ideology will conclude that it is a simple myth which corresponds to no precise reality, with the meaning more or less of a synonym for a people liberated from Hebrew and half-breed elements, and separated from its own pathologically doomed factions. Otherwise, it refers to the elites which create states and give form to nations, more or less, which is what Fascism is talking about.

Despite this, it is certain that National Socialism gives a special emphasis to the biological element, on the one hand, and to the values of loyalty, honour, and a direct and anti-bureaucratic dependence between men and men and leaders and followers on the other, limiting everything that is formalistic juridical legalism with precise political

---

140 Ludwig Ferdinand Clauss (1892–1974) was a German ethnologist who had been a student of Edmund Husserl. His idea that race was more a matter of the spirit than of biology, although still classifiable, was quite influential upon Evola. He travelled extensively in the Middle East, studying Arab culture, and he became a Muslim. Although initially hailed by the National Socialists for his advocacy of the superiority of the Nordic soul, he later fell out of favour with them since his racial theories were at odds with the Nazis' purely material definition of race, and his work was banned by them in 1942. Clauss further opposed them in more practical terms by hiding a Jewish colleague in a hidden room in his house, thus rescuing her from deportation, a deed for which he was posthumously lionised by the state of Israel.—Ed.

141 'The Doctrine of Fascism', p. 30.—Ed.

interventions. This difference, however, will tend to become increasingly attenuated after Fascism, too, has officially laid claim to the racist idea. If it follows this idea coherently, analogous values will gradually become significant among us as well, a development that will only be a benefit for our revolution, which has been blocked in so many sectors by 'positivistic', 'officious', and intellectualistic dross, and by a style, disregarding the race of the body, we cannot always call 'Aryan'.

On the other hand, it is undeniable that the National Socialism of fascist ideology will be able to receive more than one stimulus to pass from the dynamic phase, of which its views still betray the influence, to a more 'classic' phase, in which attention will be paid most especially to the objective conditions for the definition of a stable and, in its own way, 'positive' order, freed from circumstances and revolutionary developments. Perhaps the consequences of the war, once it has been won, by the very fact of assuring to Germany its vital space, will permit the marginalising of certain excuses for socialisation, in which the ideology of our ally still indulges at times for tactical reasons and for the purposes of internal propaganda. Hopefully it will encourage her to come to a clearer and more Roman conception — but at the same time more consistent with the best German tradition — of the function of dominion and *ducere*.

Hitler's Table Talks

(19 MARCH 1953)

The Italian publisher Longanesi has recently published a book entitled *Hitler's Table Talks*[142] that is advertised as presenting material which casts light on the figure of the *Führer* from a more direct and personal point of view than can be found in his various political speeches and his chief work, *Mein Kampf.*

It should be observed that these are notes taken down on everything significant that Hitler had to say on rather diverse topics during his conversations at dinner with his closest collaborators, especially at his Headquarters. These notes, however, were authorised and, indeed, extensively revised by Hitler himself because, as his *ipse dixit*,[143] they were eventually intended to serve as an orientation and directives concerning the subjects they treated. Moreover, it is important to remember — as noted in its Foreword — that, even at dinner, Hitler felt as though he were on a podium, and so the material we read here does not present a truly intimate and spontaneous character. Certainly, this book reveals various aspects of Hitler's persona, mentality, and worldview with great crudeness and, let us say it right away, the revelations are not at all to Hitler's advantage.

---

142 *Hitler's Table Talk, 1941-44: His Private Conversations* (New York: Enigma, 2000).—Ed.

143 Latin: 'he himself said it'.—Ed.

The notes refer to the period from the middle of 1941 into the following year — the period of the German military apogee, before the setback in Russia and before El Alamein, the period when the dream of Germany's continental dominion over Europe seemed very close to being realised. First of all, Hitler's views on the organisation of the future Reich are very perplexing. Everything is conceived in a crudely realistic form, technocratic and bureaucratic, 'modern', let us say, in the worst sense of the word. There is no truly spiritual reference, but a violent will to power in various artificial aspects, as when he plans a status for various populations, like the Russians, aimed at scientifically fomenting their cultural and even physical inferiority in contrast to the German groups that are meant to colonise, exploit, and dominate their lands.

The myth of the superior race is naturally the basis of such opinions, but it is the myth as it might be conceived by a dilettante, who is satisfied with vague formulations for use as simple political tools, which end up compromising what might be correct in anti-democratic doctrines. If Himmler still had a more or less precise idea in referring to the Nordic race in the strict sense, Hitler, by taking into account what is, in general, German and 'Germanic' for the most part, is not dealing so much with racism as with an inflamed nationalism. It is in fact well-known that the Germanic is a conglomerate of difference races, whose superiority to other national conglomerates is therefore more or less problematic.

If Hitler does not go beyond the horizons and sensibility of a mediocre bourgeois with a taste for Wagner in his tastes and evaluations concerning the world of art, in what concerns religion, the Church, the monarchical and dynastic idea, and the traditional nobility, it must be said that he absolutely sinks to the level of the brutality and vulgarity of a socialist proletarian in these conversations. He almost ends up defining religion, like Marx, as an opium of the people, as a means of exploitation, and as something obscurantist which the progress of science will little by little cause to disappear, to the great benefit of a regimented national community turned to purely temporal greatness.

It is well-known how recurrent Hitler's references to Providence were, whose designate, protector, and executor he felt himself to be. It is difficult to understand what this Providence could mean for Hitler, when, on the one hand, he recognises the right of the stronger as the supreme law of life with Darwinian triviality, while, on the other hand, he excludes any supernatural intervention or order as superstition, and asserts 'the impotence of man before the eternal law of nature', as in the most obsolete and outdated scientism.

There is no lack of interesting and intelligent observations on various concrete problems in this book. The general atmosphere, however, is very different from the one that could correspond to a true leader, and who could be legitimately invested with absolute authority.

Ritter,[144] who was in charge of the German edition of the work, writes at the end of his Introduction that the lesson to be learned from it is that the reason for the defeat was not the superiority of the enemy's war potential, nor the delay in preparing a secret weapon, and not even the presumed sabotage by the forces of the resistance. 'The man himself and his system carried in themselves their condemnation.' Despite all that we have said in this review, we do not agree with these words. It is strange that a German would say them. A German ought to know that Hitler essentially acted as a centre of crystallisation for very diverse forces, which were united under the sign of the swastika only in order to confront unavoidable problems of internal and external politics. These forces were in no way crated by National Socialism, but received their form from an earlier, higher tradition. System and ideas

---

144 Gerhard Ritter (1888–1967) was a historian, a monarchist, and a German nationalist. Initially a supporter of the Nazis, he later became an ardent opponent, and was arrested for his participation in the 1944 assassination attempt against Hitler. After the war he continued to defend and promote German nationalism by attempting to separate it from the Nazi legacy.—Ed.

should not be confused with bogus imitations and traits due to contingent factors. Many Germans did not commit this confusion and were united with Hitler only in the name of Germany, or rather of Europe, while waiting for an eventual process of clarification and rectification that the purely military factor was doomed to cut short.

A History of the Third Reich

(1962)

The publisher Einaudi has recently published a large book entitled *The Rise and Fall of the Third Reich: A History of Nazi Germany.*[145] Since another work on the same topic by an English author, well documented and written with a certain impartiality, was published a little while ago by an important Milanese publisher,[146] the need for this new book is not obvious, had it not been for its decisively partisan character and the corresponding contribution that it makes to the deformation of recent history.

The book's author is one W L Shirer,[147] an ordinary American journalist of the most irritating and presumptuous type, who lived in Europe for a little more than twenty years, without having done any serious research, as a reporter. When he returned to America after the war, he began attacking the anti-Communist politics of the America Right after the Korean War with such animosity that he was fired by the

---

145   William L Shirer, *The Rise and Fall of the Third Reich: A History of Nazi Germany* (New York: Simon and Schuster, 1960).—Ed.

146   Evola is likely referring to Alan Bullock's *Hitler, a Study in Tyranny* (London: Odhams Press, 1952), which was published by Mondadori in Milan in 1955.—Ed.

147   William L Shirer (1904–1993) was a journalist who began covering Germany for American newspapers in the early 1930s. He was hired by Edward Murrow for CBS in 1938, and his first reportage was on Germany's annexation of Austria. He continued to report on the Third Reich, even into the early years of the Second World War, departing Germany in December 1940. In 1944 Shirer became one of the directors of the Society for the Prevention of World War III, which advocated for harsh peace terms with Germany in order to prevent her from ever becoming a military power again. Blacklisted for his Communist sympathies in 1950, he did little after the war apart from write this book.—Ed.

radio station which he had been working for. He retired to the country, and to console himself, he started writing this book. According to the Introduction to the Einaudi edition, over one and a half million copies have been sold in America.

The most pernicious trait of the book is found in its apparatus of sources, which, along with some truths mixed with mystifications, might make an impression on the inexperienced reader. The documentation comes, first of all, from the notorious trials of the Nazi leaders conducted by the Allies. Even American jurists have come around to acknowledging their absurdity and questionable procedure. Shirer also used diaries and the archives of the German government and the army, which the Americans sequestered, and so these records were exposed to every sort of manipulation and arbitrary, unchecked misuse. In his Preface, Shirer confesses, 'No doubt my own prejudices, which inevitably spring from my experience and make-up, creep through the pages of this book from time to time', because 'I detest totalitarian dictatorships in principle'.[148] How, then, can he claim at the same time to be 'severely objective, letting the facts speak for themselves and noting the source for each'?[149] Everyone knows that facts and sources never speak for themselves. Everything depends on choosing them and the light in which they are placed. In this case, the light is very much from the Left.

Shirer's animosity is seen (not least) in his delight in trivial epithets that would repel any serious historian: the 'fat' and 'effeminate Field Marshal' (Goering), the 'oily hack' (Rosenberg), the 'arrogant' and 'insufferable' Ribbentrop, the 'drunken stutterer' (Ley), the 'sawdust Roman Caesar', the 'big breasted' (or 'bloated') Italian dictator (Mussolini), aside from the recurring and insulting use of the term 'gangster' (not always kept in the Italian translation) for the leaders of

---

148 *The Rise and Fall of the Third Reich*, p. xii.—Ed.

149 Ibid.—Ed.

the Third Reich: a rather imprudent insult, since Hitler had already emphasised that this term was created in America to describe a phenomenon for which America can take full credit.

There is no need to point out that Shirer, who detests 'totalitarian dictators in principle', casts an indulgent veil over the Soviet version, as he does not speak of the horrors committed by the Communist regime and the Red Army as soon as they had the upper hand. It is significant that he writes in the Introduction that he sees in the Third Reich 'the last of the empires which set out on the path taken earlier by France, Rome and Macedonia',[150] placing Hitler on the same level as Alexander, Caesar, and Napoleon. This association, while it values Hitler more than his due, reveals the bitter contempt which this journalist and radio broadcaster from the United States has for the greatest figures of European history.

There is no room here to detail all the elements that are misrepresented and downright falsified in this book. What Shirer says about the 'Intellectual Roots of the Third Reich' demonstrates, for instance, a ridiculous lack of culture and an unbelievable puerility. This is especially serious, given the great importance of distinguishing the valid elements presented by the German tradition (thanks to Germany's having been largely spared the influence of the subversive ideologies of the Third Estate).[151] These elements continued to exist in Nazism (often *despite* Nazism), and constituted the positive aspect of the Third Reich. Of incidents that Shirer makes up out of whole cloth, let us limit ourselves to a few concerning Italy, since Shirer seems to despise Fascism and Mussolini even more than he does Hitler. He systematically denigrates the Italian army. For instance, the 'headlong flight of the Italians', who 'were seized by panic', is supposed to be the cause of

---

150 Ibid.—Ed.

151 In pre-Revolutionary France, the general assembly of the French government was divided into three States-General: the clergy (First), the nobles (Second), and the commoners (Third).—Ed.

the final German surrender in Russia. When did Mussolini ever have to combat 'anti-German demonstrations that broke out all over Italy' in 1943? When were there ever, in 1943, 'mass strikes in the industrial cities of Milan and Turin, where the hungry [!!!] workers had demonstrated for "bread, peace, and freedom"? (The fact is, during the Salò Republic, the industry of northern Italy functioned with perfect discipline and efficiency.) What led him to write that Mussolini 'was completely taken by surprise when, on the evening of July 25, he was summoned to the royal palace by the king, summarily dismissed from office, and carted off under arrest in an ambulance to a police station'? (The fact is, it was Mussolini who presented himself to the King and offered him his resignation.) And so on and so forth. From these few specimens one can imagine Shirer's 'scrupulousness' and 'objectivity' in many other affairs concerning Germany.

In the chapter on 'The New Order', Shirer can only repeat the old stories about atrocities, persecutions, concentration camps, the Gestapo, and so on. He implies that the world had only to expect such things from the 'New Order' in the event of an Axis victory. He does not mention the positive initiatives that the new Germany had undertaken, and skims over them in other chapters in an inadequate and disparaging fashion. The agrarian legislation for the defence and 'dignifying' of farmers, for their loyalty to land and lineage against urban proletarianisation and financial exploitation; the reconstruction of the economy with the elimination of class warfare and a new, organic, and personalised unity of the forces of labour in factories; the so-called *Ordensstaatsgedanke*,[152] that is, the ideal of a stable and anti-democratic state, protected from politics as usual and party manoeuvring, supported by something like an 'Order' (like the old Order of Teutonic Knights, the original root of the Prussian ethic), and so

---

152 In *The Path of Cinnabar*, Evola defines *Ordensstaatsgedanke* as 'a state based not on a democratic "leadership" but on an Order—an elite founded on an ideal, a tradition, an austere discipline and a common lifestyle' (p. 155).—Ed.

on — these are some of the positive elements, which are not so much due to the Nazis as they were reclaimed from an earlier and higher tradition and, if applied in the right way, could have demonstrated their salutary rectifying force in today's world. It is possible that, had a process of purification been attempted, they would have proven superior to all the problematic and negative elements presented by Nazism (or, rather, Hitlerism), the existence of which we are far from denying.

As for the 'horrors', persecutions, and so on — when they did occur — it is well to speak clearly. History and revolutions have always offered numerous examples. No one talks about the cruelties committed by the 'chosen people' during the conquest of the 'promised land', and the massacre the traditional feast of Purim still commemorates,[153] nor about the Catholic wars of religion at the start of the modern era, or the Terror in France, or the massacres of the Communist revolution and its regime. Instead, the Third Reich is made a unique and unprecedented case.

Let us say without mincing words that no price would have been too high to pay if a different outcome of the Second World War, that is, the victory of the Tripartite Pact, the Axis, had had the following consequences: breaking the back of Soviet power, probably liberating Russia from Communism and preserving all of eastern Europe from its domination; humiliating England and expelling the United States from European, if not global, politics; preventing the danger posed by Communist China, since the victory of Japan would have certainly made the rise of Mao impossible; in the climate of the 'New Order' various colonies would have probably changed patron, but there would have been men with a steady pulse to defend European prestige and

---

153 In the Book of Esther, it says that a vizier named Haman had made plans to have all the Jews residing in the Persian Empire killed because the Jewish aristocrat Mordecai refused to bow down to him, casting lots, or *purim*, to determine the date of the massacre. The Jews manage to win the support of the Persian King, and Haman is killed, after which the King grants the Jews permission to kill anyone who poses a threat to them, leading to the massacre of more than 75,000 people. Purim thus celebrates this change of fortunes.—Ed.

block the rising of the peoples of colour[154] and prevent the formation of one of the virulent sources of the crisis of a world that essentially owes its current fearful insecurity to what Churchill himself acknowledged, with tardy repentance, in the lapidary phrase: 'We have slain the wrong pig',[155] alluding to the Third Reich, instead of the Soviet Union.

Finally, the journalist Shirer's book is published by Einaudi in its series, the *Library of Historical Culture*. It is an edifying example of how the culture of 'free' Italy is manipulated with ample means.

---

154 Here, the editors of *Il Nazionale* added, 'or at least their premature and uncontrolled <rising>'.—Ed.

155 This is a comment widely attributed to Churchill, but where, when, or even if he actually said it remains undetermined.—Ed.

Hitler and the Secret Societies

(October 1971)

I t is curious that various French authors have devoted themselves to researching the relationship of German National Socialism with secret societies and initiatory organizations that are supposed to have inspired Nazism. They have even posited an 'occult background' to the Hitler movement. This thesis was first presented in the well-known book, rich in digressions, by Louis Pauwels[156] and Jacques Bergier,[157] *The Morning of the Magicians*.[158] The book defined National Socialism in terms of a union of 'magical thought' with scientific technology, and finally ends up producing a formula for it: 'battleships + René Guénon,'[159] a formula that would have made that eminent exponent of traditional thought and the esoteric disciplines spin in his grave.

The book is marred by a serious mistake, because it frequently confuses the magical element with the mythic one, although the two have nothing to do with one another. It is undeniable that 'myths' played an

---

156 Louis Pauwels (1920–1997) was a French author and journalist, and a follower of Gurdjieff, who became known in the 1960s as a writer and publisher of popular writings on occult matters and science fiction. In 1978 he began publishing the *Figaro-Magazine*, which became a forum for French New Right thinkers such as Alain de Benoist.—Ed.

157 Jacques Bergier (1912–1978) was a Russian Jew whose family fled to France following the Russian Revolution. He conducted research into nuclear physics, and then was active in the French Resistance. By the late 1950s, he had joined his friend, Louis Pauwels, in his publishing efforts. They wrote several popular books on occult topics together.—Ed.

158 *The Morning of the Magicians* (New York: Stein & Day, 1964).—Ed.

159 In the English edition of the book, the passage reads 'Hitlerism, in a sense, was "Guénonism" plus tanks.' From *The Morning of the Magicians*, p. 180.—Ed.

important role in National Socialism: the Great Reich, the charismatic Leader, race and blood, and so on. Here, however, it is necessary to give to the word 'myth' its plain, Sorelian[160] sense of a 'force-idea', an idea as a motivating force, endowed with a special suggestive power (as, in general, is true of the myths used by demagogy) with no 'magical' implication. Thus, for instance, no one will think it is reasonable to attribute a 'magical' element to the myths used by Fascism, such as the myths of Rome and the Leader, or to the myths used by the French or the Communist revolutions.

The discourse would be different when dealing with the influences of an order that is not simply human, which certain movements might have obeyed without realising it. There is no question of this, however, in the view of the French authors we have mentioned. They are not thinking of influences like this, but of concrete influences exercised by organisations that are real, although, to one degree or another, 'secret'. They even speak of 'Unknown Superiors' who are supposed to have raised up the Nazi movement and made use of Hitler as their medium. It is not clear, however, what their goal was in doing so. To judge by the results, that is, the catastrophic consequences of National Socialism, even if indirectly, for Europe, we would have to think of dark and destructive ends, which would go against the thesis of those who would like to relate the occult side of that movement to what Guénon called 'counter-initiation'. The French writers we have mentioned have proposed another thesis, which is that the medium Hitler emancipated himself from the 'Unknown Superiors' at a certain moment, like a Golem, and from that point on the Nazi movement went off in a fatal direction. In this case, however, it really must be said that these occult Superiors had possession of very limited foresight and powers, if they could not block someone they had used as their medium.

---

160 Georges Sorel (1847-1922) was a French philosopher who began as a Marxist and later developed Revolutionary Syndicalism. He advocated the use of myth and organised violence in revolutionary movements. He was influential upon both the Communist and Fascist movements.—Ed.

On a more concrete level, there has been much imagination expended on the origins of the essential themes and symbols of National Socialism with reference to pre-existing organisations, but to which, however, it is difficult to attribute an authentic and regular initiatory character. There is no doubt that Hitler did not invent Germanic racist ideology, the symbol of the swastika, or Aryan anti-Semitism, all of which had existed for quite some time in Germany. A book entitled *Der Mann, der Hitler die Ideen Gab*[161] speaks of Lanz von Liebenfels (the noble *von* was self-bestowed), an ex-Cistercian monk, who founded an order that used the swastika, and published a journal, *Ostara*, from 1905, and which Hitler certainly knew, in which Aryan racist and anti-Semitic theses were clearly articulated.

Much more relevant to the occult background of National Socialism is the role attributed to the Thule-Gesellschaft ('Thule Society').[162] Here matters become more complicated. This society was the offspring of a pre-existing Germanenorden ('Order of Germans'), which was founded in 1912 and headed by Rudolf von Sebottendorff.[163] Von Sebottendorff had lived in the East, and in 1924 he published a strange volume on the *Die Praxis der alten Türkischen Freimaurerei*,[164] in which he described procedures based on the repetition of syl-

---

161 Wilfried Daim, *The Man Who Gave Hitler his Ideas: Jörg Lanz von Liebenfels* (Munich: Isar, 1958). No English edition exists.—Ed.

162 The Thule Society was established in Munich in 1918, and sponsored the formation of the German Workers' Party, which later became Hitler's National Socialist German Workers' Party, in January 1919. However, Hitler severed the Party's links with the Society by the early 1920s, and there is little indication that it had any significant impact on Nazi ideology or strategy. The definitive work in English on it is Nicholas Goodrick-Clarke, *The Occult Roots of Nazism* (Wellingborough: Aquarian, 1985).—Ed.

163 Rudolf von Sebottendorff (1875-1945), an alias of Adam Glauer, a German who moved to Turkey and became a citizen in 1911, and who was adopted by the German aristocrat Baron Heinrich von Sebottendorff, a German aristocrat who was also living as an expatriate there. Rudolf studied Bektashi Sufism there, and then returned to Germany in 1913 to begin spreading his own mystical teachings, which led to the creation of the Thule Society. By 1920 Sebottendorff had returned to Turkey, however, and was never involved with either Thule or the Nazis again. Evola is somewhat mistaken, however, as Theodor Fritsch, not Sebottendorff, was the founder of the Germanenorden, and the Thule Society was not founded until 1918.—Ed.

164 *Practices of Ancient Turkish Freemasonry* (Leipzig: Theosophische Verlagshaus, 1924). English edition: *Secret Practices of the Sufi Freemasons: The Islamic Teachings at the Heart of Alchemy* (Rochester, Vermont: Inner Traditions, 2013).—Ed.

lables, symbols, gestures, and 'paces', the purpose of which was the initiatory transformation of the human being which is also sought in alchemy. It is not clear which Turkish 'Freemasonic' organisations von Sebottendorff was in contact with, nor whether he had practiced these rituals as well as described them.

Nor can we be sure whether they were regularly practiced in the Thule-Gesellschaft, which he directed. It would, however, be important to know this to evaluate the fact that many leading personalities in National Socialism, beginning with Hitler and Hess, were members or were in contact with it. There is no doubt that Hess was a member, and that he in turn, as it were, 'initiated' Hitler when they were together in jail after the failure of the Munich *Putsch*.

At any rate, it should be emphasised that, more than simply because it had an esoteric side, the Thule-Gesellschaft was attractive because of its appearance as a relatively secret society with the swastika as its emblem, and because it was characterised by a decidedly anti-Semitic and a Germanophilic racism. One should be cautious about supposing that the chosen name of this organisation, Thule, attests a serious and conscious reference to Nordic polar symbolism and an ambition to establish a link to the Hyperborean origins of the Indo-Germanic peoples, because primordial Tradition has counted Thule as the sacred centre or sacred isle situated in the far north. We should mention, on the other hand, the possibility of a rather more profane origin for it, since Thule can be the deformation of 'Thales', the name of a locality in Harz, where the 'Order of Germans' had organised a convention in 1914, having as its order of business the formation of a secret racist organisation to combat the forces that were supposed to exist behind international Jewry. It was especially this order of ideas that Sebottendorff emphasised in his book, which was published in

Munich in 1933, entitled *Bevor Hitler kam*,[165] to point out what myths and ideology had already existed before Hitler.

Therefore, serious research into Hitler's initiatory links to secret societies does not take us very far. As for Hitler as a medium and his magnetic force, some clarifications are necessary. That Hitler owed this force to initiatory practices seems to us pure fantasy. Otherwise, we would be in the absurd position of supposing a similar cause for the equally impressive psychic force possessed by other leaders — by Mussolini, for instance, or Napoleon. Rather, we should believe that, once a collective movement has been awakened to life, a type of psychic vortex is created which concentrates itself in anyone who is its centre so as to confer a special nimbus upon, especially for impressionable people.

As for his being a medium (which, incidentally, possesses the opposite traits of qualification for initiation), it can be acknowledged in Hitler, with certain reservations, insofar as he does appear as possessed in more than one respect. (This trait distinguishes him from Mussolini, for instance.) Precisely when he was arousing crowds into fanaticism, he gave the impression that another power had carried him away, using him exactly like a medium, even if one of a very special and exceptionally gifted type. Anyone who has heard Hitler speak to raving crowds must have had that impression. Given the reservations we have expressed concerning the supposed 'Unknown Superiors', it is not easy to determine the nature of such a super-personal force.

As for National Socialist 'gnosis', or a presumed, almost mystical and metaphysical dimension, it is necessary to remember the singular coexistence in this movement and the Third Reich of 'mythic' aspects with openly Enlightenment and even scientistic aspects. Numerous references can be found in Hitler of a worldview that is markedly 'modern', or else, basically, profane, naturalistic, and materialist, while

---

165 *Before Hitler Came* (Munich: Deukula, 1933). No English edition exists.—Ed.

at the same time he had faith in a Providence of which he believed himself to be an instrument, especially for what he regarded as the fate of the German nation. (For instance, he saw a sign of Providence in his having escaped by the skin of his teeth from the attempt on his life in his general headquarters.) Although he disregarded the myth of blood, Alfred Rosenberg, the movement's ideologue, talked about a 'mystery' of Nordic blood that had a sacramental value, but this same man, when it came to Catholicism, attacked every rite and sacrament as mystifications and, like an Enlightenment *philosophe*, took sides against the 'obscurantists of our time' and ascribed the invention of modern science to the credit of Aryan man. At the foundation of all this is the explanation that, if their attention wandered to runes, the ancient Nordic and Germanic signs, they were exhumed on a purely emblematic level, almost as happened in Fascism with certain Roman symbols which had no esoteric assumption behind them. The Nazi program to create a superior man betrayed a 'mysticism of biology', again a mainly scientistic orientation. At most it could be a question of a 'superior man' in Nietzsche's sense, but in no way in an initiatory one.

The project of the 'creation of a religious and military racist order of initiates united around a divinised leader' cannot be considered that of official Nazism, as René Alleau suggests in *Hitler et les sociétés secre`tes; enquête sur les sources occultes du Nazism.*[166] Among others, he referred to the Islamic Ismailis[167] as antecedents. It is rather in the context of the SS, which, take note, was established in a second period of the Third Reich and that held a position within it that displayed some motif of a higher plane.

---

166 *Hitler and the Secret Societies: The Occult Origins of Nazism* (Paris: Grasset, 1969). No English edition exists.—Ed.

167 The Ismailis are a branch of Shi'a Islam who adhere to an esoteric interpretation of the religion. They are perhaps best known for having given rise to the Hashishin, or Assassins, who terrorised their opponents among Sunni Muslims and the Christian Crusaders through targeted assassinations between the eleventh and thirteenth centuries.—Ed.

Especially in the intentions of its organiser, Heinrich Himmler, the SS was clearly meant to create an Order that aimed at education according to the Prussian ethic and the ethic of the ancient chivalric orders, especially the Order of Teutonic Knights. For this kind of organisation, Himmler sought a legitimation or chrism, which, however, he could not draw from Catholicism, as did the old Orders, because the Church was openly opposed by the radical current within Nazism. Even without the possibility of any sort of traditional link, Himmler referred to the Nordic and Hyperborean (Thule) legacy and its symbolism. These references were not due to the 'secret societies', of which we have spoken, but instead looked (as Rosenberg had also done) to the research of a Dutchman, Herman Wirth,[168] who studied the Nordic and Atlantic tradition. (Wirth received subventions from an office created for him by Himmler, the Ahnenerbe.)[169] This is not without interest, but there is no sign of 'occult backgrounds'.

So the overall balance is negative. The limit of the French authors' ramblings is established by J M Angebert, *Hitler et la tradition cathare*.[170] At centre stage are the Albigensians (or Cathars),[171] a sect of heretics that was widespread in southern France between the tenth and twelfth centuries, and which had its capitol at the fortress of Monségur. It was destroyed, according to Otto Rahn,[172] in a 'crusade against the

---

168 Herman Wirth (1885–1981) was a Dutch German who believed that there was an ancient, worldwide Nordic culture which had been forgotten apart from some traces which remain encoded in ancient myths and symbols. Like Evola, he was briefly involved with the SS Ahnenerbe in the 1930s.—Ed.

169 The Ahnenerbe, or 'ancestral inheritance', was a special branch of the SS established in 1935 to research the history, archaeology, and anthropology of the Germanic and Aryan peoples.—Ed.

170 *Hitler and the Cathar Tradition* (Paris: Laffont, 1971). English edition: *The Occult and the Third Reich: The Mystical Origins of Nazism and the Search for the Holy Grail* (New York: Macmillan, 1974).—Ed.

171 The Cathars believed that the God as represented in the Old and New Testaments were actually different gods, with the God of the New Testament being the God of goodness and of the world of the spirit, whereas the God of the Old Testament was the God of evil who had created the material world.—Ed.

172 Otto Rahn (1904–1939) was a German researcher who was fascinated by the mythos of the Holy Grail, and he made many explorations, particularly in southern France, in pursuit of it. He unenthusiastically joined the SS in 1936 as a way to earn a living and support his research. He froze to death in Austria in 1939, and it is still debated whether he committed suicide or was murdered.—Ed.

Grail', (which is the title of his book, *Kreuzzug gegen den Gral*).[173] It is completely obscure what the Grail has to do with the Templars and this sect, which was characterised by a type of fanatical Manicheism[174] in flight from the word and which was the enemy of earthly existence in flesh and matter, to the degree that its followers let themselves die of hunger or committed suicide by other means. (We corresponded with Rahn and tried to show him the arbitrary nature of his thesis.) It has been suggested that Rahn was in the SS and that a German expedition was sent to discover the mythical object that was supposedly rescued at the time of the destruction of the Cathar fortress at Monségur. The object was supposed to have been guarded during the Third Reich. After the fall of Berlin, a division had opened a path all the way to Zillertal, near the Italian border, taking this object with them in order to hide it at the foot of a glacier, in expectation of a new era.

In reality, there was talk of a commando who seems to have had a less mystical mission, saving and hiding the Reich's treasure. Two other examples of where imagination can lead when its reins are loosened and it is carried away by *idees fixes*:[175] the SS (which included not only military units but also scholarly specialists and so forth) organised an expedition to Tibet for mountaineering and ethnological purposes, and another expedition to the Arctic, apparently for exploration and also for the eventual creation of military bases. According to these fantastic interpretations, the first expedition was supposed to have been seeking to establish a link with a secret centre of Tradition, while the second was aiming at contact with the occult, hyperborean Thule.

---

173 *Crusade Against the Grail* (Freiburg: Urban, 1933). English edition: *Crusade Against the Grail: The Struggle Between the Cathars, the Templars, and the Church of Rome* (Rochester, Vermont: Inner Traditions, 2006).—Ed.

174 In ancient Persia, the Manichean religion taught that the entire cosmos was locked in combat between forces of absolute good and evil.—Ed.

175 French: 'obsessive idea'.—Ed.

INDEX

OTHER BOOKS PUBLISHED BY ARKTOS

OTHER BOOKS PUBLISHED BY ARKTOS

PORUS HOMI HAVEWALA	*The Saga of the Aryan Race*
RACHEL HAYWIRE	*The New Reaction*
LARS HOLGER HOLM	*Hiding in Broad Daylight* *Homo Maximus* *The Owls of Afrasiab*
ALEXANDER JACOB	*De Naturae Natura*
PETER KING	*Keeping Things Close: Essays on* *the Conservative Disposition*
LUDWIG KLAGES	*The Biocentric Worldview* *Cosmogonic Reflections: Selected* *Aphorisms from Ludwig Klages*
PIERRE KREBS	*Fighting for the Essence*
PENTTI LINKOLA	*Can Life Prevail?*
H. P. LOVECRAFT	*The Conservative*
BRIAN ANSE PATRICK	*The NRA and the Media* *Rise of the Anti-Media* *The Ten Commandments* *of Propaganda* *Zombology*
TITO PERDUE	*Morning Crafts*
RAIDO	*A Handbook of Traditional Living*
STEVEN J. ROSEN	*The Agni and the Ecstasy* *The Jedi in the Lotus*

OTHER BOOKS PUBLISHED BY ARKTOS

RICHARD RUDGLEY

Barbarians

Essential Substances

Wildest Dreams

ERNST VON SALOMON

It Cannot Be Stormed

The Outlaws

TROY SOUTHGATE

Tradition & Revolution

OSWALD SPENGLER

Man and Technics

TOMISLAV SUNIC

Against Democracy and Equality

ABIR TAHA

Defining Terrorism: The End of Double Standards

Nietzsche's Coming God, or the Redemption of the Divine

Verses of Light

BAL GANGADHAR TILAK

The Arctic Home in the Vedas

DOMINIQUE VENNER

The Shock of History

MARKUS WILLINGER

A Europe of Nations

Generation Identity

DAVID J. WINGFIELD (ED.)

The Initiate: Journal of Traditional Studies

CPSIA information can be obtained
at www.ICGtesting.com
Printed in the USA
LVHW091253140119
603833LV00001B/52/P